F-Bomb Affirmations

rewire your brain and become the kickass human you were born to be

Natalie Stokell

Published by Change Empire Books

www.changeempire.com

All rights reserved

Printed on demand in Australia, United States and United Kingdom

Edited & designed by Change Empire Books

This book is sold subject to the condition that it shall not, by way of trade or otherwise, be lent, resold, hired out, or otherwise circulated without the publisher's prior consent in any form of binding or cover other than that in which it is published and without a similar condition including this condition being imposed on the subsequent purchaser.

The scanning, uploading, and distribution of this book via the internet or via any other means without the permission of the publisher is illegal and punishable by law. Please purchase only authorised electronic editions and do not participate in or encourage electronic piracy of copyrightable materials. Your support of the authors' rights is appreciated.

While the authors have made every effort to provide accurate internet addresses at the time of publication, neither the publisher nor the authors assume any responsibility for errors or for changes that occur after publication. Furthermore, the publisher does not have any control over and does not assume any responsibility for author or third-party websites or their content.

EBOOK ISBN: 978-0-6487453-9-6

PRINT ISBN: 978-0-6488138-0-4

For Skyla and Star. You light up my world and I love you beyond measure. May you always know your worth and may your life be filled with an abundance of 'fuck yes' moments.

CONTENTS

The Beginning 007

Part One 025
   1. Istanbul and Brain Science 101 027
   2. Beliefs 045
   3. The One About Robots and Chickens 063
   4. Creating a Bridge Between Your Feeling Brain and Your Thinking Brain 075

Part Two 089
   5. 'It Is Safe…' 091
   6. 'I Am Allowed…' 110
   7. 'I Am Worthy…' 130
   8. 'I Am Grateful…' 148
   9. 'I Am So Fucking…' 170

The End, But It's Really Just The Beginning 193

Gimme More 199

Acknowledgments 200

THE BEGINNING

1 'Excuse me, excuse me.' I push my way through the crowd of groupies cluttering the courtyard by the backstage door. There's some jostling as they hesitate, reluctant to give up the precious spots where they've been waiting for who knows how long.

They turn to look at me, at first with disdain – and then, upon seeing what I'm carrying, disdain grudgingly turns to understanding and envy.

Fuck, this is awkward.

I start to feel nauseated. I can't believe I am doing this. Maybe I should turn back.

Who the fuck do I think I am? I don't belong here.

Every cell in my body wants to run, but I resist the urge to turn around and instead continue to put one foot in front of the other, slowly moving through the group towards the front.

Come on, Natalie. Breathe. Use your tools.

I'm having a mental block, and it takes me a moment to run through my usual coping tactics.

Okay, an affirmation.

I keep moving forward.

I've got this. I've got this. I've got this.

Nausea still rises. But I keep breathing. Then it dawns on me: now would be a great time to test my new theory about affirmations.

Okay. I've fucking got this. I've fucking got this. I've fucking got this.

Focusing on the power the extra word gives the affirmation, the stormy ocean that is my belly calms, and my energy and confidence surge. I soon reach the front few rows of fans; now I can see the security dude guarding the door. He's massive and looks like he crushes butterflies for fun.

Shit. Perhaps I should go back? What the fuck am I doing?

But I can only imagine what the groupies' faces will look like if I turn around. I'm such a people pleaser that the mere thought of their faces, unimpressed by my failure, drives me on.

No. I've fucking got this. I've fucking got this. I've fucking got this.

I push through the last of them. The ones at the front are the hardcore fans; they've probably been here since early this morning. I expect them to resist. But they part for me, as if out of respect that I've made it this far.

Butterfly crusher sees me and raises an eyebrow.

Okay, game on. Come on. I can fucking do this.

'Hi,' I say. 'Um, I'm here for Justin Timberlake.' The lie feels clunky in my mouth.

Butterfly crusher says nothing, and so I turn my body slightly so he can see what I'm carrying.

'Oh, right.' He looks relieved. He's probably dealt with a few too many obsessed groupies in his time. 'For massage. Sure, come on in.'

A rush of endorphins flood my body as I realise that's the first gatekeeper down.

Hell yes, I've fucking got this.

He pushes open the doors, and after manoeuvring myself and my table through them, I find myself at the end of a very long corridor with multiple doors. I recognise the familiar warren of backstage.

Ah, shite, where to now?

I turn back to the closing doors. Seeing my questioning face, Butterfly Crusher catches a door and holds it open. 'It's Joey you'll be wanting, the tour manager. He's at the end on the left, name on his door.'

'Thank you!' I smile in relief.

Yep, I've fucking got this.

I walk with confidence into the depths of backstage.

I can hear what's possibly a sound check going on in the belly of the building. There's a buzz of pre-show adrenaline in the air. People dressed predominantly in black jeans with oversized black tees and sporting hair overdue for a haircut nod at me and say hello in voices out of an American sitcom. I smile and return the greeting, feeling a bit like I am in an American sitcom myself.

The last door on the left has an askew laminated sign attached to it reading 'Joey'. I try not to look too closely at the naked cartoon man that someone has drawn in the corner.

The door is ajar, but I knock anyway.

'Yep, come in!' the sitcom voice calls from within. I push open the door to find a man sitting behind a makeshift desk, wearing – surprise! – a black t-shirt and in need of a haircut.

'Hey, Joey,' I say, 'I'm checking in to see if anyone's needing massage tonight.'

Please don't let this be all in vain.

'Oh yeah, cool, sure.' Joey gets to his feet. 'Let me find you a space to set up in. That would be great.'

Boom, second gatekeeper down! Hell yeah, I've fucking got this.

Joey finds me a small room that's not in use and I set up, putting out some of my own laminated signs to direct people to me.

I wish I could tell you that I did in fact get my hands on Justin Timberlake that night, but it was mainly crew and his band. Big American roadies who asked for deep pressure and then took it back when they felt my strength, making jokes about how they hadn't realised they'd be beaten up by a woman today. And small, toned dancers, their overworked bodies hungry for a therapeutic touch.

I left that evening with my pockets full of cash and, more importantly, my confidence flying. Not only had I done something completely out of my comfort zone – I had nailed it.

Back when I lived in London, I massaged musicians backstage and celebrities in their penthouses weekly, through the company I was contracted to. Here in Australia, I didn't have the backing of the company, and I missed the work and the money. When I heard Justin Timberlake was playing Brisbane, I wondered who of my colleagues might have been assigned to him in London. Then

I thought why not me, here, in Australia? Could I just turn up and wing it?

This thought reflected the shift which had been happening within me recently. Since becoming a mother, I'd found my fierce. The lioness within me had awakened: the mama bear, the protector.

This fierceness was echoed in my journaling, my thoughts, in the workings of my inner world, and now it was manifesting in my outer world. I was doing things I hadn't thought myself capable of.

And I started colouring all parts of my life with this shift. This mama was claiming her space in the world. This mama was making shit happen.

Specifically, my affirmations. I had started dropping an F-bomb into my affirmations.

And fuck, did it work! My affirmations felt stronger, fiercer, more reachable. It was like giving them a turbo boost.

They felt awesome.

But let's back-track for a moment. Let's go back to when I first found and fell in love with affirmations. Let's go back to that decade when Paula Abdul was playing on every ghetto blaster, and no top was complete without shoulder pads.

Let's go back to the late '80s.

'I get $40 a month,' Amelia Packham said, 'and I just buy whatever clothes I want.'

The rest of us stared at her, and then the awestruck responses came, tumbling over each other:

'What? That's so cool!'

'I wish my parents would do that.'

'You're soooo lucky.'

The nine girls in my class were getting ready for our weekly swim classes in the tiny, unheated concrete pool that our equally tiny school was proud to have.

I was at that age where I was painfully aware that I wasn't 'cool.' Even though I was wearing the same cycle shorts as the cool girls – complete with neon embellishments – the aura of 'cool' still eluded me.

However, in the damp, chlorine-heavy changing room in our varying states of undress, the boundaries of cool were loosened. That late summer afternoon, we were all chatting together, the three 'cool' girls and the six not so cool.

As I stood on the cold, painted concrete floor of the changing room, my head spun as Amelia, the coolest of the cool, revealed that parents gave her a clothes allowance – that she got to buy her own clothes.

A clothing allowance... Imagine being in charge of buying my own clothes.

Armed with this revelation, I went home that night and presented the case to my parents.

'You don't have to buy my clothes or take me shopping anymore,' I told them. 'Just the monthly clothing allowance, and I'll do it all.'

To my amazement, they agreed.

That weekend, I caught the number 14 bus into town to spend my first clothes allowance. This was the '80s: kids had a long leash back then.

I went to Cuba Street and walked that strip, smiling like the cat that got the fucking cream.

Some new stonewash jeans, or a cropped oversize tee?

Then a word in a window caught my eye. A word that will forever be my weakness:

BOOKS

I looked up at the sign above the shop window: Christopher's Crystals.

Books and crystals – two of my favourite things! What kind of books would a crystal shop have?

I paused, thinking about the stonewash jeans.

Oh, I'll just have a quick look.

Books had long been my escape from reality.

And my reality of late was something I wanted to escape more often. My mother had been diagnosed with lupus a few years earlier and was in and out of intensive care for weeks at a time. She was also visited by the black dog of depression for months on end. We had a plethora of nannies and home help during those in between times, but getting lost in a book allowed me to disengage and exist in a world of happily ever afters.

I entered the shop and scanned the shelves of salt lamps and Buddha statues until I found the shelves containing the books. I ran my finger along their spines, my eyes and mind cracking open at the titles: *Astral Travel, How to Lucid Dream, Pagan Rituals*.

I had never seen anything like this. Magic was a big part of my life, but it was the party trick kind of magic, not the magic these books seemed to be alluding to the magic of things unseen.

My brothers and I were brought up Catholic by our mother. Our father, a non-believer, used to stand at the front door on a Sunday morning waving and saying with a sparkle in his eye, 'Say "Hi" to Jesus from me.'

If Catholicism was my mother's religion, then magic was my father's. He was a hobby magician, and his pockets were always bulging with handkerchiefs and coins that he would whip out to entertain and delight.

However, I knew from a very young age that the church wasn't my space. God in the Catholic sense didn't ring true for me. And it may or may not have reached the point where our mother had to bribe us by stopping at the corner store for a 50-cent mixture after church.

While the stifling rules of the church repelled me, I still connected to the concept of God. The idea of an unseen power we could talk to resonated with me.

And the idea of magic, of the impossible being possible, also resonated with me on a deep level.

Both of these ideas melded into a strange cocktail of belief and wonder.

It was about the same time as I began rebelling against going to church that my father started showing me how some of his magic tricks were done.

While a part of me was thrilled to be let in on the secrets, there was another part of me which was so let down it wasn't in fact 'real magic.' And by the time I resisted church, the whole 'God thing' had been tarnished by it, and I was unable to develop my own relationship with that universal and higher power I knew existed but that had been reduced to 'God.'

Without either of these things, I was left yearning. Yearning for that sense of possibility and connection with a greater power.

I knew it existed, but something didn't sit right with me.

If I could only access 'God' via the stifling rules of the church, and if magic wasn't real, then what was?

Coming across a whole corner of books about these topics reignited the part of me that yearned to connect with magic and the unseen power. Any stonewash-tinted thoughts swiftly disappeared as I realised that with $40 burning a hole in my pocket, some of these books could come home with me instead of said stonewash.

I left with four books, one about dreams, one about crystals, one about astral travel, and one about affirmations – yes, I had picked up *You Can Heal Your Life* by Louise Hay, published a few years earlier.

When I got home, I brushed off any questions about my new clothes and shut myself in my room for the rest of the weekend. I couldn't tell you much about the other books, but reading the affirmation book felt like an orchestra of light bulbs popping in my head.

It just made so much sense to me. The mind–body connection. It confirmed what I always knew about there being more to this world than that which we can see with our eyes.

And it spoke to that part of me which yearned for magic to be true. To the whisper inside who said, 'Oh yes, anything is possible,' and to that longing for my reality to be more than 'an ill mother, three younger brothers to care for, and a magic yet emotionally absent father.'

This was the beginning of my love for learning about all things mind–body connection, mindset, and mindset tools like affirmations.

This fascination lasted into my teens, and I decided to study psychology at University. I soaked up everything I could about our brains and their development, and how that affects our interaction with the world. But after five years of study I was ready for some 'real world' living, so I packed my rucksack and left my mamaland for the adventures of Europe.

As I travelled and played, I dabbled in using my mindset tools...but I was pretty distracted by boys with French accents and £10 flights to cities I had never heard of. It wasn't until years later, when I was pregnant, that I committed to affirmations in a big way.

I looked down in the water and there was a head sticking out of my vagina.

What the actual fuck?

This was so surreal. I felt a bit detached. Emotionally numb. My body rested between contractions. In the stillness, my thinking brain awoke.

That's my child.

Where was the ring of fire? The tearing in two?

The tiny part of my brain not engaged in the moment nodded sagely and reminded me that I'd made this happen, that all the work I'd done had made my birth the way it was. The birthing sensations were intense, but I didn't experience them as pain.

I had approached birth like an exam. An exam I needed to nail. Just as in the late '80s, I had once again spent more money on books than clothes, but this time opted for pregnancy books over crystal books and maternity clothes over stonewash. I read anything and everything I could about birth. And somewhere along the way I stumbled on this thing called HypnoBirthing.

There were amazing birth videos on YouTube where the mamas just smiled serenely through birth in a candle-lit room with a soundtrack of dolphin music. This piqued my curiosity, and after finding out more – and perhaps the practical logisicts of birthing with dolphins in Hawaii – I enrolled in an online HypnoBirthing course.

Soon I was learning about how to use hypnosis to essentially repair the brainwashing by mainstream media telling us that birth is awful and painful. The mind–body connection and the power of the mind... Yes! This was my kind of language.

A big part of the course was listening to affirmations daily. I loved them so much that I listened to them most nights, too. They soothed any fears I had around birth, gave me permission to spend time thinking about the kind of birth I wanted, and felt so good when I repeated them back.

And now, in a birth pool in our living room, they were paying off.

I felt the next push in my body and, not consciously engaging with it or pushing myself, I just let my body do its thing. And my baby slipped out of me and into the arms of Pete, her daddy. He gently lifted her out of the water and onto my chest.

She was quiet, but wide eyed and alert.

I had done it.

I might not have been as quiet as all those hypnobirths that I watched on YouTube, and I might not have noticed the dolphin soundtrack that Pete put on, but I had a beautiful, straightforward, and easy birth.

And, most importantly, my biggest fears, around pain and the feeling of 'splitting in two,' weren't realised.

Sure, I felt the intensity of the pushing, but the sensations were exactly that: they were intense, a full pressure. There was no burn, no 'ring of fire.' In fact, I felt kind of numb around my whole vagina. The 'natural anaesthesia' I had been affirming daily had come into effect. Thank you, HypnoBirthing.

A few months later, deep in the postnatal haze of heart-cracking open love and sleep deprivation, I realised I was missing doing my daily affirmations. Mamahood was busy and exhausting, and I found myself needing mental stimulation. So, while I was elbow deep in nappies and stuffing breastpads down my bra, I began to wonder what would happen if I applied my affirmations to other areas of my life like I had for the birth. Life could perhaps become pretty epic.

I invested in a microphone and began recording some affirmations for myself. I started with affirmations for postnatal recovery and positive thinking. I wrote a list of affirmations, made some gentle music, and then recorded the affirmations over the music.

Recording affirmations became my sanity among the daily grind that is being a full-time mama. When our daughter was down for the night, or when Pete took her, I set up my laptop and microphone and created affirmation tracks.

Soon I had more tracks than I knew what to do with – they almost took on a life of their own. They wanted to be made available to the world. They wanted to be touching other people's lives. They wanted their own website.

And so the 'Affirmation Boutique' was born.

I made a few sales and started blogging and adding to my library of tracks. Each track was 2–3 minutes long; the idea was that someone could pick the areas of their life they were working on and choose a few tracks to create a 10-minute playlist to listen to daily, or nightly while they were sleeping.

But then I found myself pregnant again, and my site got hacked. Of course, nothing was backed up, and starting from scratch was too overwhelming for this mama.

I turned to my middle brother for advice – the TED-talking, workaholic, fun-loving, social change passionate brother.

'Upload them to SoundCloud,' he told me.

'What? For free? All this time and effort for free?' I was shocked at the idea.

He sighed in empathy and then said tentatively, 'Well, when are you going to be able to do a new website?'

'Well...' I paused to keep my toddler from feeding her baby sister raisins and caught sight of the piles of washing, half-full snack plates, and toys strewn chaotically across the once tidy floor. 'Yeah, it's probably going to be a little while,' I admitted. 'Life is pretty busy right now.'

And so, disheartened and sleep deprived, I reasoned that at least with SoundCloud my creations would be out there, helping the people I had created them for in the first place.

Five years later, both my 'babies' were now in school and I began playing with affirmations again. I logged into my SoundCloud account for the first time since uploading the original files and stared at the numbers on the screen.

That can't be right, surely?

A swarm of butterflies started to dance in my solar plexus, and the corners of my mouth twitched upwards.

Six fucking figures.

I blinked a few times, refocused on the screen, bit my lip, and slowly re-read it.

219,317 plays

219,317 freaking plays of my tracks!

The smile escaped from my lips in a laugh and the butterflies took flight.

That's 219,317 times that my affirmation tracks have been listened to on SoundCloud.

Well, I'll be damned! Thank you, brother!

My little affirmation tracks, created during 'naptimes' from my bedroom studio, had 219,317 plays.

This was the sign I needed. The little nudge I was on the right track in wanting to revisit and rework my affirmations.

My 'baby' was now 5 and the toddler 8, so I had the space to look at my affirmations again.

The new affirmations I began to work on were quite different from the ones I had done in the past – in fact, quite different from any affirmations anyone had ever done.

Giving birth and entering motherhood was a profound experience, and for me it epitomised the mind–body connection. Birth is a very physiological process, and it also feels very magical.

Creating and growing and birthing a human is pretty miraculous. No matter how that baby is conceived – whether via the old-fashioned way of horizontal dancing or via medical assistance – and no matter how it is birthed – either with dolphins off the coast of the Red Sea or in surgical theatre – it is magic. Growing a person, a whole freaking person, is pretty much straight-up magic.

And for me, birth both tapped into my power and connected me with the energy of the miraculous. It was the beginning of my journey into finding my fierce as a woman. Of letting go of my 'nice girl' and stepping into my 'strong woman'.

And I wanted this for my daughters. I wanted them to be rooted securely in the world, and to know that there was much more than the world would ever tell them.

I wanted them to have the tools and 'know how' to stay positive in a place that can sometimes feel dark and scary.

I wanted my daughters to have a strong foundation of belief in themselves and confidence in their engagement with the world.

I knew the key was in the mind–body connection. But I also knew that something was missing.

Why did my affirmations only work some of the time? Why did I have an 'easy natural birth' but not the wealth I desired? Why was I in good health but not driving my dream car? Why was I with an awesome partner but still renting rather than owning a home? These were, quite possibly literally, the million-dollar questions.

And so, packing lunch boxes with one hand and wielding a microphone in the other, I started tinkering with my affirmations and exploring what made some of them work and others not.

In between cutting another effing piece of toast into 'triangles not squares' and doing another effing load of washing, I researched, I journaled, and I tested.

I read everything I could on affirmations, on limiting beliefs, and on the power of our brains.

And then I tweaked my affirmations and tested them on myself, journaling daily about the results.

Then one day at the park, while lost in the meditative back and forth of my daughters on the swings, everything crystallised, and I realised that it all boiled down to five keys. I had five ways of hacking my affirmations. Five ways of working with the limitations of my brain – and its limitlessness, too.

And here we are.

This book shares with you my five keys to 'hacking' your affirmations.

But, more than this, I want these pages to be the 'proof' of that magic you already know is possible.

I want the facts and studies that I share with you to back up that feeling inside – you know the whisper that tells you that you *can* do it, that more *is* possible, that your dreams *are* within your reach.

That's what this crazy life is about. It's about having the best experience of yourself that you can, getting out of your own way and loving yourself enough to allow the unfurling and blossoming of your highest potential.

And yes, this can sound 'woo woo,' but by the end of this book you will see that it is in fact rooted in logic and supported by science.

We are funny beings, we humans. Even though we all quietly have a deep knowledge of and belief in our own greatness, we constantly doubt this and seek proof of the fact. We know in our heart of hearts that we are in a world of possibility, and we believe that a better future and better version of ourselves do exist. We just don't know how to access it.

It is my intention that by the end of this book you will understand how your brain works, and you will know how to *work* your brain. The first part of the book gives you a very basic understanding of brain science. It will provide you with the proof, the hard data, the facts, and the research to back up that inner whisper trying to tell you of your awesomeness. It is important you understand this, as it will be the supporting information for the second part.

Once you have this under your belt and you understand how your brain works, then you'll be nice and ready to dive into the second part of the book – the juicy part that will help you step into and liberate your awesomeness.

In this second part of the book, I will explain the five keys, and you will be able to begin applying them straightaway to who you want to be and the things you want to do and have in your life.

Everything is possible. Your dreams are within your reach. And you've got what it takes.

Let's do this!

PART ONE

1
ISTANBUL AND BRAIN SCIENCE 101

Taking a deep breath, I pushed open the cold metal door and stepped into an airless, overheated room. The smell hit me first: nappies only changed twice a day and clothes in need of a good wash.

The heavy door and the high-walled perimeter, only accessible by a guarded entrance, made the government-run compound feel like a military base. The buildings were painted a sickly pale yellow, and the windows were high and few. Each building held a different age group.

The toddler building was the one I was drawn to most. I had initially done a few days in the baby building, but I felt my heart break a little each time I went in there. The sea of cots, bottles propped up on pillows, the silence as if they had given up crying – it was all too much for me. So I had settled into a weekly routine of visiting the toddlers.

A dozen or so little heads had turned upon hearing the door open, and seeing it was me, they started to get up and toddle in my direction, desperate for human touch and comfort. A few were smiling, most were weary, almost jaded, and some just locked eyes with me as if to keep me from leaving. Soon the others caught on that I was there and I was quickly swarmed.

The staff had made themselves scarce, most likely relishing the opportunity for a break themselves, so I was alone with around 30 little humans.

I pulled the bottle of bubbles from my pocket, unscrewed the top, and then lifted and blew. This delighted and distracted enough of them that I was able to sit down on the floor, and the few that wanted cuddles more than bubbles climbed on my lap and snuggled into my sides.

As I blew bubbles and cuddled, I let my eyes travel to the edges of the room.

Shit, I wish he wouldn't do that.

My eyes had focused on a little boy, of no more than 2, who was violently banging his head against the wall.

Oh, fuck, there's another.

In the corner, another child knocked her head rhythmically against the wall. It was a softer bang, but she was going at a faster pace. My heart clenched at the sight. I focused on my breathing, keeping it slow and steady, battling with the part of me which wanted to run from the room.

Even though I was witnessing what I had learnt in theory during the five long years of my master's in psychology, seeing it in the flesh was always distressing. I didn't think I would ever get used to witnessing it.

Rationally, I knew they were self-soothing.

I knew they were head-banging to get the dopamine hit in their brains. The repetitive and intense motion released a 'feelgood' neurochemical cocktail for these feelgood-starved children. And this cocktail was worth the pain of the head-banging. It was likely their receptivity to the feelgood cocktail resulted in them experiencing pain as the others were my touch – as something comforting and soothing. And so, head-banging was what they did to override the stress of their situation.

Sadly, I also knew that these children would be the ones susceptible to opioid drug abuse later on in life. Given that their brains were primed at such a young age to seek dopamine to feel better, dopamine would become their coping mechanism in a world unable to meet their basic emotional needs.

It was their way of surviving.

I shifted my attention back to the tiny warm bodies leaning into mine and to the delight on the faces of those enjoying the bubbles. This was why I came. To plant some seeds of delight. To give these little bodies some love and affection.

I could feel the little bodies settling into me as they started to relax. I knew that it all counted. Every little moment of love and laughter, every bit of feelgood, every smile... It all helped their developing brains.

But I understood why many of the expats who volunteered at this orphanage in Istanbul found it too hard to return after the first few times.

The following week I was at the Hamam with Katya – a lithe, 20-something Dane – for the traditional bathhouse experience, which we'd become slightly addicted to. Katya was in Istanbul with her husband, who was contracted to a big construction company. Like many expat women, Katya looked like she had just stepped off the catwalk, but she was the sweetest person underneath the Prada veneer. She'd been going to the orphanages for a while.

'It's so hard, isn't it?' she said. We were lying on the hot stones in the bathhouse, our bodies being scrubbed raw by elderly maternal attendants, themselves naked bar the small sarongs tied around their waists. 'I mean, I know it's good for the kids to have us visit,' Katya continued. 'But I feel so depressed and helpless when I leave.'

'I know,' I replied, trying to avoid the huge, swinging breasts of the leather-skinned Turkish grandmother as she briskly swiped the loofah across my shoulders. I focused my attention on Katya and added, 'It's hard to leave them there isn't it, and go back to our normal lives.'

'Suzy has stopped going,' Katya said. 'I think it was too hard on her.'

Suzy was a bird-like Texan who had recently arrived in Istanbul. Bird-like both in nature – flighty, nervous – and in stature – petite and tiny-limbed. I knew she'd been struggling with culture shock in general, so visiting the orphanage probably pushed her well past her comfort zone.

'Oh, that's a shame,' I said. 'When I called Annalisa, she said she hasn't been in a few weeks, either.'

'I guess it feels too hard, too distressing.' Katya sighed. 'I know how they feel.'

'I know it's hard, but it's so important. The way our brains develop is "experience dependent." So...' I paused as Katya raised her head and cocked an eyebrow questioning. 'Oh. Experience dependent means that how our brain forms depends on what experiences we have.'

'Okay...' She nodded and then turned onto her other side at the prompting of the attendant so the rest of her body could be scrubbed and lathered.

'If we don't have certain experiences,' I explained, 'then certain parts of our brains don't develop. So, the more good experiences we can give these kids, the better it is for their brain development.' I paused to check that Katya was following. 'I know these visits feel small in the scheme of things, but honestly they can make such a difference.'

'Oh wow,' Katya said. 'Okay, so there could be long-term effects of our time there?'

'Yes, totally!'

'Maybe you should tell the others about this?' she suggested. 'I think it would help.'

Once the pendulum-breasted attendants were satisfied that we were as smooth and as clean as possible, we tipped them, got dressed, and said our goodbyes until next time. I went for a drink at one of the cafes in the back streets near the Grand Bazar. I opened my notebook and started writing a presentation to give to the group of expats.

Two weeks later, I stood at the head of a massive dining table. Seated around it were the expat ladies – and many were ladies in the true sense of the word. Dressed in beige and pearls, most were here supporting their husbands in their careers. Unable to work, they were free to volunteer their time. Staff quietly moved around the table, serving us afternoon tea, and the sea of Gucci-clad, kind-hearted women, many of whom were twice my age, awaited my expertise.

I wanted them to have hope and to feel positive about their visits to the orphanage. But most of all, I wanted them to keep showing up. I wanted those warm little bodies and developing brains to feel connected and loved, to feel seen and held. I wanted their brains to store these experiences. I wanted neurons to fire in the parts of their brains that learn about relationships, empathy, and love. I wanted these little forgotten children to be given a chance at a better life when they were old enough to leave this place.

I took a deep breath and started.

'I know how hard it can be visiting the orphanage,' I said. 'How it can make us feel helpless and sometimes even useless – like our visits aren't actually doing anything in the grand scheme of things.'

There were multiple nods around the table – sad, resigned nods from Suzy, Annalise, and the others, and a big, smiling nod of encouragement from Katya.

'But our brains develop according to what experiences we have,' I continued, 'and recent research shows that in even the most unfortunate conditions, positive interactions can actually impact our brain's development.'

I could see heads start to tilt to the side in understanding and eyes light up a little as they heard me quote the studies to back up my words. I explained about the critical periods for development and what a good thing our visits actually were. I wanted them to know that their visits had a positive impact. That every bit helped.

'So,' I said, drawing my presentation to a close, 'even just a few hours of positive experiences a week can positively impact and change the brains of the children.' I smiled and stepped back, signalling I was finished speaking.

The talk was well received. Afterwards, a few of the women came up to me and expressed their gratitude.

'I feel so much better about my time there now,' said one, her eyes bright with optimism. 'Thank you.'

'Yes, it's like there is hope,' added another, smiling and nodding enthusiastically. 'Like my time can make a difference there.'

I felt much better, too. Hope was back.

And a healthy dose of hope and knowledge might just ensure that many of those little developing brains were exposed to some of the experiences they needed to grow into healthy, happy humans.

My time at that orphanage in Istanbul was where theory and real life met. After completing my master's degree, I was so close to applying for a PhD…but I was scared I would end up existing in an academic bubble. I was hungry for the real world.

So much of what I had learnt from textbooks was played out before my eyes as I travelled, but it wasn't until Istanbul that I realised the real-world impact of all the theory.

Istanbul allowed me to see the significance of my studies on the brain's plasticity – and those darling, head-banging children were indisputable proof that the brain is wired for survival.

★

We are biological beings. No matter how spiritual or intellectual you might feel, there is no way around it – we are flesh, blood, and guts. Sure, we have consciousness and can reach states which transcend our body – horizontal dancing, anyone? But essentially, we are a bunch of thoughts walking around in a skin suit.

But nature is pretty fucking awesome. She gets things RIGHT. She wouldn't tease us with all this amazing equipment without some pretty epic software to go with it!

She wants us to survive and perhaps even to thrive in the world.

As biological beings, we are primed for survival. All the organs in our body play a vital role in our survival; our lungs to gather and then send oxygen to our bloodstream, our hearts to send that oxygen to our cells, our brains to assess our environment, and our reproductive organs to ensure the survival of the species.

And like most of our body parts, we just let our organs do their 'thang' while we live our lives.

A key part of survival involves learning from and being in harmony with our environment. This is the domain of the brain. This is also the one organ that we can engage with pretty meaningfully on a daily basis. The one organ we really shouldn't just let do its 'thang.'

So, while it might not be sexy, it is important we start with a brief overview of how the brain works. At the end of this chapter, you will understand some basic geography of the brain and the biological reasoning behind why it is the way it is.

Once you have a grasp on the epic power of your brain, you'll see what your brain can do for you if you are in the driver's seat, rather than merely a passenger with your brain at the wheel.

Instead of passively watching the scenery go by, looking yearningly at beach after beach of beauty and then stopping in the middle of the night at some random petrol station, you'll be the one deciding which route to take, which party to stop at – *'hello, full moon party'* – and which to give a miss – *'pity party, no thanks.'*

Knowledge is power, and knowing the science behind how your brain works will help you to understand your own agency.

Sometimes we feel like our life is just happening around us, and we can feel helpless.

But *you* can be in control of your life and in control of your brain rather than it controlling *you.*

At this point, I know that some of you may be thinking, 'Ah crap, science…' You may want to tune out or skip this bit, but while it is neuroscience, you do not need to be a scientist to understand this.

Let me say that again:

You do not need to be a scientist.

I am going to keep this super simple and easy to understand. If you do find your inner geek loving and nerding out over this, then I can point you in the right direction for additional neuroscience, but for now let's keep it simple.

I will also include at the end of each chapter a 'tl;dr' ('too long; didn't read') cliff notes version of the most important points you need to understand before moving to the next chapter.

We'll start our lesson with a brief description of the parts of the brain. I want to preface this by saying that the brain is part of a really complex system, one that we're going to reduce, for our purposes, to much simpler and easier-to-understand concepts. Then we'll discover how the body communicates with itself and take a closer look at how our brains develop in childhood. Lastly, we will see how the brain creates shortcuts to more efficiently analyse the world.

Brain Science 101

Have you ever walked into a room and immediately sensed that something was up? There's tension in the air, and you feel like you just walked in on an unfinished argument or the prelude to the orgy?

Our brains take in *everything* that we sense, even if we're not conscious of it.

We read body language – hell, we probably read hormones, too.

The key is to make sure that we feed the brain with helpful information as well.

Firstly, allow me to introduce you to three significant parts of your brain, and then we will focus on the two most relevant to us:

1. Your reptilian brain

    This was the first part of your brain to develop back when we were evolving as a species and is thus known as the reptilian brain. It is the most primitive part of the brain and is responsible for basic life support functions like regulating our heart rate and breathing, movement, and spatial orientation. It is a very small, densely packed part of the brain, right at the top of your spinal cord.

2. Your mammalian brain

   Also known as the midbrain, limbic, chemical brain, or emotional brain. This part of our brain helps to regulate our internal states, such as temperature, blood pressure, digestion, hormone levels, and so on. This part of your brain is also responsible for what we call the four Fs – fighting, fleeing, feeding, and fucking – and for the 'flight or fight' response to stress.

   For our purposes, we'll stick with the F theme – some of my favourite words begin with an F – and we will refer to this as your *feeling brain*.

3. Your neocortex

   The third part of the brain is called the neocortex. This part of the brain is what differentiates us from reptiles and mammals. This is what makes us human. This is the area responsible for the higher functions of thinking and reasoning.

   For our purposes, we'll refer to this as your *thinking brain*.

In this book, we'll concern ourselves with the *feeling* and *thinking* brains.

All the parts of the brain engage with each other, and the brain communicates with the rest of the body via different communication systems.

Remember, an accurate assessment of the environment is key to our survival, but doing so continually and consciously would be extremely fatiguing. So, our *feeling* brain does it for us and then sends the info we need to know to our *thinking* brain to interpret and to act on.

Communication Systems 101

While we have many communication systems in the body, three of the main ones are the nervous system, the endocrine system, and the immune system.

The nervous system includes the spinal cord, the brain, and all the nerves which carry information between our bodies and our brains. This information is carried on neurotransmitters. Neurotransmitters are chemical messengers; think of them like carrier pigeons, carrying information throughout the body.

A key part of the nervous system is the autonomic nervous system. It has two parts: the sympathetic and parasympathetic. The sympathetic system is the part engaged in the 'flight or fight' response to stress, while the parasympathetic part is engaged when the body is in rest and relaxation.

The endocrine system includes all the hormonal centres of the body and the hormone molecules. This is a slower system than the nervous system. This means it takes longer for a message to reach the body from the brain via this system.

Lastly, there is the immune system, which is the internal communication network that signals damage to cells or the presence of foreign organisms or chemicals in the body. It lets the body know when disease is present.

All of these systems can interact with each other.

As we go about our day, different stimuli in our environment will activate cells in parts of our *feeling* brain. Neurotransmitters are released, and once they flood the brain, a corresponding emotional state is produced. This emotional state then changes the body.

Then, and only then, these physiological changes are transmitted back to the brain and the feelings are registered by our *thinking* brain. It is only at this stage that there is some thought or analysis of the situation and stimuli.

Up to this point, everything takes place in the *feeling* brain.

For example, we might be lost in that meditative state of driving on a long stretch of familiar road. A kangaroo leaps on to the road in front of us. Our eyes register this, and first to respond is our *feeling* brain: a burst of adrenaline floods the body, and our muscles tense. This is then interpreted by the *thinking* brain: 'Oh, shit, a roo, I don't want to hit it!' And we slam our foot on the brakes or swerve to avoid it. The *feeling* brain engages first, followed by a corresponding physiological reaction in our body, and then our *thinking* brain engages with its interpretation of the situation.

Another example might be walking the into our house after a long day and being faced with a floor full of school bags, shoes, papers – a plethora of 'other people's stuff.' We see it, and the sight is sent to our *feeling* brain. For some of us, this corresponds with tension in the body, and this tension is then sent back to our *thinking* brain for us to analyse the situation: 'Ah, shite, what a mess. Damn it, why can't they pick up after themselves...'

For others, the analysis might happen like this: it is sent to our *feeling* brain, but there are no corresponding emotions, and so we classify the situation as 'life as normal,' with no stressful accompanying thoughts.

From the perspective of biological survival, it is only once our *thinking* brain receives information that there is some analysis of the situation. Additionally, the initial assessment in our t*hinking* brain primarily focuses around 'Do I want more of this? Or less of this? Which will ensure my survival?'

Brain Waves 101

Human children are very vulnerable when they are born, and their first years are dedicated to learning all about their environment so they can survive in it. Animals, on the other hand, are born at a much more developed state, ready to walk and to run from predators if need be.

Thus, the human brain needs to be in a highly receptive state for learning in our early years, so it can quickly learn how to survive in the world. The more receptive the brain is, the easier it is for the brain to store information about the environment.

A key to receptivity is brain waves, something you've likely heard of in some context. Brain waves are patterns of neural activity in the brain, patterns of the neurons communicating with each other. Depending upon the needs of the 'user', these patterns are either fast or slow.

Two of the most receptive brain wave states for learning are delta and theta. In adults, delta waves usually only occur in sleep or meditation. In children, delta is the dominant state until around 2 or 3 years old.

Have you ever noticed how, when someone has taken a mind-altering substance, they can become quite childlike in their interaction with the world?

'Whoa, check out that ladybug, man! So colourful, and the perfection of those spots!'

Sounds a bit like,

'Wow Mama! Look at dat ladybug! Pwetty spots!'

You can picture them both, can't you? The 20-something stoner bending to look at the ladybug on a leaf, his Calvin Kleins showing above his low-slung, well-loved Levi's, and the squatting toddler, hands resting on chubby thighs – both gazing with the same wonder and awe in their voice.

This is because they are both in delta, or even theta, states. Delta and theta states are states of openness and awe, states of readiness to have your mind blown open – states in which you're very suggestible because your brain is ready to learn. Whether you're under the influence of a mind-altering substance or you're in those receptive years of early childhood, brain waves impact how you interact with the world.

In delta, your brain waves and neural activity are slow, which makes it very easy for your brain to take on new information and create new neural pathways.

This, of course, is why there's so much emphasis on childhood development.

Let's return for a moment to those darlings in Istanbul. For some of them, the situation was just too much, and so in order to survive they needed to create some 'feelgood.' They needed to create an experience which overrode their current experience. Head banging releases serotonin, endorphins, and dopamine. This *internal* chemical rush was enough to create feelings to override their *external* situation.

And while this behaviour is dysfunctional, it perversely serves the function of providing the child with the feelgood it needs at that moment.

However, the head-banging behaviour and subsequent dopamine rush, combined with the suggestible state of delta and neglect, cause the brain to wire in a way that may cause problems later in life.

Brain Shortcuts 101

As the brain starts to learn about its environment, it stores what it has learned as shortcuts. It wouldn't be very effective to re-learn the environment each time; in creating these shortcuts, the next time the brain registers the same stimuli, it will already know what to expect or how to react.

When neurons fire together, they wire together. This wiring becomes the shortcut and can be thought of as a 'known' about the environment. Instead of having to re-learn all the things all the time, the brain effectively stores information about the environment so this information is easy to access the next time.

The more often the same neurons fire together, the stronger the wiring becomes.

While our clever, clever brain and its time- and energy-saving shortcuts are awesome, for the most part, there are times that these shortcuts actually do not serve us.

The sweet orphans in Istanbul are a perfect, albeit extreme, example of how information gathered about our environment that is intended to help us survive can, in the long run, actually hinder our lives. A long-term side effect of the specific neurons wiring in the head-banging children is the susceptibility of this child to later seek other means of achieving a dopamine rush – such as opioid drug use.

Sure, in the moment these children are 'surviving.' However, the shortcuts created to survive in the moment go on to inform how we move in and engage with the world long beyond that moment.

The brain favours surviving in the short term over thriving in the long term.

Neuroplasticity 101

You might be thinking that this sounds a little hopeless – but wait! There's hope! While the shortcuts created to help us survive in the world impact how we interact with the world on an ongoing basis, they are not set in stone.

It used to be thought that once the brain had wired in certain ways, that that was it. But now we know that the brain has 'plasticity,' even beyond the important childhood years.

Plasticity means that we can create new neural pathways and disrupt old ones. We can fire and wire new neurons and make new connections.

In further chapters, I will go into this in greater detail. For now, just know that your brain is one awesome creation.

And that's our brief, simplified brain science for now. In the next chapter, I will discuss how our brain can be a bit 'connection happy' and start making lots of shortcuts. Many of these shortcuts are not helpful in the long term.

However, you have at your service an amazing organ, and once you understand how you can work its nuances to your advantage… Well, the world is your oyster.

And pearls you can make!

Too Long; Didn't Read

- Our brains develop in relationship to our world and our circumstances.
- The brain's primary function is to ensure our survival. Like the captain of a ship, it assesses the journey along the way and adjusts the course as necessary.
- There are two main parts of the brain that we will refer to throughout this book, and we will simply call them the *feeling* brain and the *thinking* brain.
- Information reaches our *feeling* brain before our *thinking* brain.
- Our brain waves in childhood make us very receptive to learning about the world.
- As we learn about the world, our brain gathers information and stores its findings.
- In an effort to be efficient, it stores these findings as shortcuts.
- While our shortcuts inform how we see the world, they aren't set in stone; we can change them well beyond the childhood years.
- Your brain is amazing. Be amazed.

2

BELIEFS
THE GOOD, THE BAD, AND THE UGLY

With one hand at his lower back, which troubles him when it's cold, the elderly man shuffles to the other side of the laboratory, tweaking the end of his waxed white moustache with his free hand. He picks up the bell, focusing his eyes on his subjects, then rings it with a quick flick of his wrist. His subjects' ears twitch, and he leans in closer to the device attached to their jaws. He picks up his quill, dips it in ink, and scratches some numbers in the ledger in the middle of his cluttered and dust-covered desk.

'Ivan?' a woman calls from the next room.

The man keeps writing and then looks out his window at a field obscured by morning fog. He doesn't notice the view, but his eyes move as his brain kicks into gear.

'Ivan?!' The voice is louder now, with an air of impatience.

Still in deep thought, the man twists the ends of his moustache.

'Ivan Petrovich Pavlov!' She strides into the room. 'Your breakfast is ready!'

Ivan looks up in surprise, and then smiles upon seeing her. Her gaze softens and she repeats herself, but this time with a smile of her own.

'Your breakfast is ready.'

'Thank you, dear.' He returns her smile. 'Were you calling me? I was a little lost with the dogs.'

Still smiling, she shakes her head and reaches out her hand.

And, with one hand on his back and the other in her hand, they shuffle out of the room together.

You've probably heard of Pavlov's dogs. This is how I imagine Pavlov: a frail, skinny white dude with a waxed moustache. He lives a quiet life with his doting wife and dogs, and even though it's the 1900s, he writes with a quill.

Wikipedia shows me he actually had a full beard and his moustache wasn't waxed; he looked rather well fed, actually, and with four children, I imagine his life wasn't that quiet.

He was an animal lover, though. And he was one of the first researchers in his time to work with animals in a relatively humane way, extracting his results while keeping them alive rather than by vivisection.

With a passion for science from childhood, Pavlov became one of Russia's most renowned scientists, but he is best known for his findings with dogs.

Originally, Pavlov was researching the digestive processes of dogs. However, after observing that their saliva glands were activated by the mere presence of the technician who fed them, rather than the presence of the food itself, Pavlov pivoted his research. He started ringing a bell each time he fed his dogs. The dogs quickly learnt that the bell meant food. And, soon enough, he was able just to ring the bell to get their salivary glands going.

Their biology created a shortcut in their brains. Their brains made an association between the sound and the arrival of food. The sound itself became their cue to prepare for food.

Pavlov's dogs are a classic example of neurons firing and wiring together, as we discussed in the last chapter. The neurons that registered the sound of the bell fired and wired to the neurons that produce saliva. The ringing of the bell made the dogs produce saliva regardless of whether food was coming or not.

However, research with dogs was limited because there was no way to know what they were thinking. So, let's take this one step further and hypothesise that if the dogs were merely to think of food, their glands would probably be activated, too.

This is where studies on humans are more interesting, because we can ask about conscious thoughts, or encourage thoughts of something and see what happens in the brains when the human subjects think about it.

This is evident in simple things, for example, thinking about certain food.

I want you to think of a lemon.

A beautiful, sunshine-yellow lemon.

Now, imagine cutting a wedge out of that lemon. See the juice spray out as the knife cuts through the skin and into the flesh.

And now, imagine holding the wedge to your nose and smelling the sharp tang of the juice. Then see yourself taking the wedge and putting it in your mouth...

At which point did your mouth start to water? Your brain thought that you were having a lemon. Your brain was told, 'incoming lemon,' and the receptors for saliva started to fire. Pretty cool, hey?

Your ever-so-clever brain doesn't know the difference between an experience that is really happening and an experience that is happening inside your head. The thought of the experience and the actual experience itself both produce the same effect. Both send messages to your body to prepare for the incoming experience – e.g. a sour lemon inside your mouth!

Yes, the exact same neurons fire in your brain whether you're actually having an experience in real life or just thinking about the experience.

And in this chapter, I am going to show you that it's possible to use this to your advantage.

But first, we will discuss how the different wirings in your brain can be either helpful or unhelpful. I'll explain how a one-time analysis of the world as well as a repetition of something can both become so strongly wired that they become belief. We'll talk about how these beliefs can affect our very biology.

Then I'll begin to tell you how you can start to consciously use this knowledge to your favour, to create the life you desire.

I want to prove to you that you are a powerful being.

I want you to KNOW that you are in fact a powerful being – powerful beyond all the woo woo, beyond all the 'love and light' – all that good stuff. You are powerful on a very real, very physiological, scientifically undeniable level.

Boom. Let's go!

We could think of our life as one big Pavlovian experiment.

However, unlike those dogs, we have a choice. We can either be super conscious of this process and work it to our advantage, or we can just roll with it like the dogs.

Because, as we learnt in the last chapter, while our clever, clever brain, with its time- and energy-saving shortcuts, is for the most part awesome, there are times these shortcuts actually do not serve us. In these times, we might in fact say that our brain is less than awesome.

Put simply:

- Our brains condition themselves to our environment.
- This conditioning and wiring of neural networks become our belief system.
- These neural shortcuts are what form our beliefs and expectations about the world.

Of course, our beliefs have been formed by our efficient brain with regard to ensuring our survival, but these same beliefs may not encourage us to thrive in the long term. While many of our beliefs are helpful, some are not. And there is a big difference between surviving and thriving.

You see, as these shortcuts quickly become beliefs about the world, they become gospel according to our brains. And, as many theologians will tell you, the trick with gospel is to see the message beyond the actual details. But our *feeling* brain isn't capable of that and instead takes the details as facts.

This is problematic when something that happened once becomes the shortcut for that experience, leading us to begin to apply it to all other similar experiences in the future.

Imagine, for example, if the first red food we ever ate was a chilli. And our brain made the shortcut that every red food made our mouth burn and our eyes water. Think of all the amazing foods we would miss out on if we kept this belief throughout our lives – strawberries, cherries, tomatoes.

Or imagine that our first relationship ended in heartbreak because our partner cheated on us, and our brain made the shortcut that all men/women/people we were attracted to are a-holes? Imagine all the beautiful people we would miss out on in our life.

In these examples, a one-time analysis of our experience of the world becomes a belief about any future experiences of the world.

And this is where we need to become conscious of shortcuts that are not in fact helpful.

How Are Beliefs Formed in Adulthood?

Remember that in order to survive in the world, our brains need to learn quickly about our environment in our early years. And it is in childhood, when the brain is in its highly receptive state, that many of our beliefs are formed.

This is not to say that we can't and don't form new beliefs in adulthood, just that the conditions need to be right.

There are three main ways beliefs are formed when we are adults:

1. When we are in a suggestible brain state – such as hypnosis or altered brain wave states.
2. When we experience a strong emotion.
3. When the same neurons are continually firing and wiring together – e.g. repetition.

An example of all three occurs in intimate relationships.

To illustrate this point, let's go back in time again, this time to the late '90s.

Clutching Annie's arm with one hand and my dress in the other so it didn't drag through the sticky, alcohol-coated dance floor, we slowly made our way to the bar. Annie was hiccupping and trying to talk, and each time she was interrupted by a loud hiccup, we both laughed.

'Woah, look, there's Lauren.' Annie stopped and I followed her pointing finger with my eyes. 'With that dickhead still.'

'Annie!' I laughed.

'Well, he is!'

'I know.' Suddenly sober, I remembered who Lauren used to be before she met him: loud, bubbly, always up for fun, but also so academically focused. She held a national-level archery medal. She was one of the most focused people I knew – or she used to be, before she met that dickhead.

'Let's go say "Hi!"'

And we pivoted and moved over.

'Hey, Lauren!' Annie said. 'Hey, Ma' – hiccup – 'tt, Matt!'

Matt managed a tight-lipped smile, his jawline pulsing like he wanted to say something. He didn't seem amused by Annie's hiccups like we were.

'Ladies,' he said, arching an eyebrow at our drunken state.

Lauren didn't say anything; her smile was also tight, but I was sure her eyes flickered with warmth before she caught herself and looked to Matt, like a child caught misbehaving. An awkward silence descended.

'Um, are you having fun?' I asked, directing my question at Lauren.

Matt didn't give her a chance to answer for herself. 'Well, you know,' he said, 'it's the usual suspects. A law ball isn't much different from a night at the Captain Cook, but everyone is just dressed nicer.'

We looked around; it was true. But there was something in the way he said it that felt more condescending than funny, and the awkwardness ramped up a notch.

I stared at Lauren, remembering the fun we used to have, the nights of beers and flirting at the Captain Cook, the days of rolling joints and smoking the hangovers away. She opened her mouth to say something, but again Matt got in first.

'Well, see you guys around.' And then he was off, pulling Lauren along by the hand. But as they went, I saw that they weren't actually holding hands; he had her by the wrist.

'That was weird,' I said once Annie and I were alone.

'Yep,' she agreed. 'He's an asshole!'

'Do you think she's okay?'

Annie didn't answer the question, instead saying, 'She was so quiet, wasn't she?'

Later that night as I was at the bar waiting for only God knew how many shots of tequila, I heard some commotion behind me. I turned and saw Lauren and Matt.

He was yelling at her, and even though I was too far away to hear the words, I could tell by their body language and his angry gesturing at the half-empty drink in his hand and the full one in hers that his drink had been spilt and somehow it was her fault.

Her face was frozen in fear and she leaned back as he spat words at her. When he stopped talking, she dropped to the floor and started mopping at his shoes and trousers with the hem of her dress. *Her dress!* He lifted her by the elbow and kind of dragged her out.

I grabbed my tray full of shots and followed. He went into the toilet, presumably to try to dry himself a little; she waited outside, looking at the floor.

'Lauren, are you okay?' I asked.

She looked a little embarrassed to see me, and so without saying anything I did what any good student would do and handed her a shot and wedge of lemon. We both did one swiftly. Then I handed her another.

A bit of colour came into her cheeks.

'What the fuck just happened?!' The tequila made me ask.

'I know, I'm just so clumsy...' Her words trailed off miserably.

'Clumsy?!' I said, spraying her with tequila and lemon. 'You are a national archery champion! You are the least clumsy person I know!'

'It's just, well, I mean, around Matt... I'm so clumsy.' She whispered the last bit, as if he might hear her from the bathroom, 'Matt says that...'

The tequila was loosening my lips and I felt a surge of hot anger. On a roll, I said, 'Is he telling you that you're clumsy?'

She looked like a deer caught in headlights and started to open her mouth. I held my hand up to stop her and passed her another drink and a lemon wedge. We both did the shot, wincing together at the lemon.

'What the actual fuck, Lauren? Look,' I said, 'you're freaking awesome, but you have turned into a shadow of yourself around Matt, who is, quite frankly' – I paused for another shot – 'a dickhead.'

She looked pained and I wondered if I had taken it too far.

'I'm sorry,' I continue, 'I'm sure he has some nice moments, but I don't think they're enough. You deserve so much better, Lauren!'

She swallowed and her chest shuddered like she was trying not to cry.

'Whether he meant to or not, I think he's made you less shiny,' I said, trying to explain. 'Maybe he was intimidated by your sparkle, and he wasn't comfortable around you? And maybe he thought he was loving you. But I miss the old Lauren. The one who laughed lots and who held my hair when I spewed.'

The alcohol was making me emotional, and I could feel the last two shots catching up to me.

She took a deep breath, looking like she was going to say something, and then her eyes flickered in alarm at something behind me. I turned, and there he was, coming back from the bathroom.

I wanted to grab her hand and pull her into the crowd. I wanted to dance and drink and laugh like we used to. But I could see that I'd already lost her. So I put my empty shot glass on the tray, and when Matt came, I smiled and gave her the biggest hug.

'You are freaking awesome, Lauren,' I whispered into her ear before walking back onto the sticky alcohol-covered dance floor.

I wish I could tell you that she called me a week later, all 'Oh you were so right, and that is just what I needed to hear.' But she didn't.

I reached out to her a few times and left messages, but she never replied.

It wasn't until the beginning of the following year, when I started volunteering at a rape crisis call line, that I was able to understand the situation a little more than I had at the law ball. In the training, we looked at the psychology of domestic abuse.

During the heightened hormones of the first flush of love, our brains create conditions for connection and bonding. Perhaps from an evolutionary perspective this is necessary so you and your mate can become 'on the same page', on the same wavelength. So I realised now that – his narcissistic tendencies aside – the hormones produced from falling in love made her brain extra suggestable to what he was saying.

And it wasn't things that might be said in a healthy romantic relationship: 'You're so great... I love the way you...' Instead, she was hearing 'You're so clumsy... It's your fault...' And these things became her beliefs about herself.

Was her brain just doing its 'thang'?

Yes.

Were those beliefs helping her to survive in the short term?

Also yes, because if she didn't agree with him, then their relationship was unstable and threatened, and there was a part of her primed to avoid this at all costs.

Were those beliefs helping her to thrive in the long term?

Definitely not.

Remember, your body is a finely tuned biological system. Your brain is primed to learn – and in certain conditions, your brainwaves ensure your brain is especially receptive to firing and wiring.

While generally this firing and wiring serves us in the current situation, some of it does not serve us later in life.

This is because your *feeling* brain does not discriminate between something that is a 'good' experience and something that is a 'bad' experience.

It is only your *thinking* brain that makes that distinction. To your *feeling* brain, it's just an experience, and it creates a shortcut to make your life easier and ensure your survival.

However, if we create a brain shortcut that isn't actually helpful, it can become problematic. That shortcut could be a belief about ourselves, like Lauren, or it could be a belief about the world around us – like 'All the people I am attracted to are a-holes.'

Is Your Past Helpful?

If we see the world through the lenses of our beliefs, does this mean that we see the world as it is? Or as we are?

Remember, it's your brain's job to keep you 'safe' and to make sense of the world. Anything that is unknown is by default considered unsafe – this is how our brain is primed. When we create shortcuts to help us make sense of the world, the shortcuts are based on past experiences. Essentially, what this means is that we make sense of the world based on what has come before us, that is, what is in fact our past.

Our beliefs are the filters through which we view the world. Our beliefs change what we perceive. And given that our *past* experiences are recorded in our brains as shortcuts, really we are being informed about our *current* reality based on our past.

Can you see how this could be limiting and keep us in the realm of doubt, inability, and 'can't' instead of the realms of potential, possibility, and 'can'?

I don't think it's possible to see the world as it is; we will always see it as we are. But imagine if our beliefs were formed from possibility, informed by the potential of our future rather than the limits of our past. What would the world, or our world, look like then?

Imagine if, when we were children, we were filled with limitless beliefs about ourselves and the world. Imagine if, as grownups, we began to feed our brains with limitless beliefs about ourselves and the world.

Imagine.

Our only limit is ourselves.

How the Fuck Can a 'Little 'Ole Belief' Affect Our Actual Physiology?

So, we know that our brains make 'helpful' shortcuts, and that sometimes the shortcuts aren't all that helpful. But these shortcuts are more than just an emotional response triggered by our beliefs. These shortcuts can affect our very biology, too. They can literally change the way our cells communicate with each other!

Perhaps the most classic example of this is the placebo effect.

You may have heard this term bandied about in pop science, or as a reason to discredit some controversial study results. But the placebo phenomenon is well documented, and it is pretty freaking amazing.

It was first coined by Henry K. Beecher in 1955 – although according to Wikipedia, the word was first recorded as used in a medical context in 1811. Beecher published a paper called 'The Powerful Placebo' in which he argued for the clinical importance of the placebo effect.

Today, not only does research take the placebo effect into consideration, but we also have a plethora of research on the placebo effect itself – from studies where people recovered from a fake knee operation to experiments where sugar pills were more effective than antidepressants!

The Oxford Dictionary definition of a placebo is:

a beneficial effect produced by a placebo drug or treatment, which cannot be attributed to the properties of the placebo itself, and must therefore be due to the patient's belief in that treatment.

In addition to the placebo effect, there is also the nocebo effect:

a detrimental effect on health produced by psychological or psychosomatic factors such as negative expectations of treatment or prognosis, origin 1960s from Latin, literally 'I shall cause harm,' from nocere 'to harm' on the pattern of placebo.

The most extreme examples of the nocebo effect are the results of receiving curses in cultures that have a strong belief in witch doctors and voodoo. There are documented cases of people getting sick and even dying after being on the receiving end of a curse.

There are documented effects of words from cultural 'authority figures' like local witch doctors, voodoo priests, or oncologists which can change the outcome of a person's health, and in some cases their life.

Does the Placebo Effect Mean That We Don't Believe in Our *Own* Power?

I'm sure you'll agree that it's kind of fucked that our bodies are capable of amazing things when they are 'tricked' into believing it. When we're told something, especially by a perceived authority figure, we can give it so much weight that our biology changes. Yet, if we told ourselves that same thing it would hold less weight and our biology wouldn't change.

The placebo effect is when we believe that something *outside* of ourselves affects us, when really it is the *belief itself* that is creating the change. For example, there are many studies that demonstrate a sugar pill can be just as effective as medication if the patient is told the pill is in fact medication. It is not the sugar pill that is making us better; it is the belief that has an effect.

What does it say about us, as empowered beings, that we have the power but don't believe that we do?

Why is it only when this belief is attributed to something else that we 'allow' it to happen?

You can cure yourself of this disease.

Versus

These pills will cure you of this disease.

To me, the placebo effect indicates the extent to which we don't believe in our own power, the extent to which we externalise our success.

Why do we struggle to step into our power and realise that we are in fact beings of power?

An alternative argument takes a more philosophical approach and postulates that to know power, we must first know powerlessness.

Perhaps.

Either way, the important point I'm trying to make here is that you are a powerful being. As the amazing Dr Joe Dispenza says, 'You are the placebo.'

So, dear reader – and yes, I am talking to you, the magic and powerful being in the skin suit reading this now. Yes, you. Let this be a reminder that you are fucking powerful!

The more you tap into that knowledge and the more you know and believe it, the more powerful and knowledgeable you will be. It's like a cycle.

And that, my lovely, is the whole point of this book! I want you to KNOW that you are a powerful being – powerful beyond all the woo woo, all the law of attraction stuff. Powerful on a very real, physiological, scientifically undeniable level.

Once you know this, then you can really work it to your advantage. In the second part of the book, we'll dive into the practical ways you can work this in your favour. But first, I want to show you that as well as affecting our biology, our beliefs can actually affect the world around us, too – and not in a perceptible way, but in a tangible way. The next chapter blows my mind just a little.

So, deep breaths...and prepare to have your mind blown.

Too Long; Didn't Read

- The shortcuts formed as our brain makes sense of the world then become our beliefs.
- Sometimes the shortcuts are helpful to us; other times they are not.
- The brain doesn't distinguish between shortcuts/beliefs that are good for us and those that are bad for us.

- The same neurons fire in our brain when we think about an experience and when we have the experience.
- Our beliefs inform our physiology.
- In adulthood, we need certain conditions to make new beliefs.
- The placebo and nocebo effects are examples of how effective our beliefs are.
- But YOU are the placebo, and you are powerful.

3

THE ONE ABOUT ROBOTS AND CHICKENS

I stood at the bottom of the garden and held the water-stained, curled-edge picture up against the view of our house.

The similarities were striking.

The same shaped eaves on both.

The same Queensland-style deck surrounding the whole house.

The big, sloping lawn leading up to the house.

And, if I moved slightly to the left, the same effing tree in front of the view!

What the actual fuck!?

This was one of those movie moments, and the next frame should have been me turning to my partner and clinking our champagne glasses with smug smiles.

But Pete doesn't drink and my 5-year-old was yelling from the bathroom, 'Maaamaaaaa! I need some toilet paper!'

The water-stained picture was from our vision board of nine years earlier. We used to keep it on the inside of one of our kitchen cupboards in our tiny ground floor London flat. The GFC had just hit, and jobless and with a new-born, we were dreaming of moving to Australia.

I had googled 'Australian houses' and then printed out the ones we liked. I'd also printed out pictures of avocado and mango trees, two of my favourite foods that tended to be bland and far from ripe when I bought them from my local fruit store in North West London.

I sat in that little flat, looking at the bullet-grey sky outside and listening to the trains rumbling by the end of our tiny garden every five minutes, to the thud of drum and bass from the flat upstairs, and I dreamed of such a house. I imagined picking fresh avocados and mangos and watching our daughter play in a garden that was train-free and bigger than a postage stamp.

It was a tough time. Pete couldn't find work, and London felt like it was getting greyer, so we decided to take the leap and leave the overcast skies of the UK for the sunny bluer ones of Australia.

And nine years later, I was standing in front of our new house with that picture from our London days.

The way we found this house was pretty magic.

We had just returned from a trip to the UK. It was our first time back there as a family since we'd left. And so it was a total whirlwind, squeezing as much as we could into the long summer days. There were family gatherings in Kent, friend hangs in the West End, glamping at a music festival, and a child-free, three-day date in Santorini. Once we got back to Australia, we were tired and jet-lagged AF.

Two days after our return, it was Pete's birthday. We had dropped the girls at school and were getting a coffee before his regular chiro appointment.

'So, what would you like to do today, birthday boy?' I asked.

'I don't know,' he said. 'I kind of feel like buying something big.'

I raised my eyebrows.

'Like maybe a car.'

Oh, Lordy, this could end badly.

'Um, what about a house instead?' I said, only half joking, since we'd been occasionally looking at houses, and I'd much rather invest in a home of our own than a car.

Pete went to his appointment and I sat by the river and hopped on my phone. It had been a while since I looked at real estate listings, but I found a few which met our requirements and started a shortlist.

Fifty minutes later, Pete floated out of his appointment and I showed him a few of the houses. The first was one of those 'price upon application' ones. I suspected it was a bit beyond our budget, but Pete picked up the phone and called.

Into seven figures – it was completely out of our range.

'Have you seen the one in Eerwah Vale?' the agent asked.

Funnily enough, the Eerwah Vale one was also on our list, and she said we could view it that very afternoon.

We pulled into the curving tree- and fern-lined driveway and came to the house as we rounded the corner. Big palms hung protectively over the path leading to the house, and a welcoming front door opened onto the porch. The agent let us in and after some handshakes and small talk led us into the lounge.

Wow, what a view!

The floor-to-ceiling windows framed the view beautifully. Rolling fields, trees, and in the distance Mount Cooroy.

We were taken from room to room.

Four bedrooms, check. Ensuite, check. Two living areas, check. Bath, check.

Then the agent took us outside and left us to wander around.

We walked down the sloping lawn, around the fire pit to the lily-covered dam, then across past the vege patch to the chicken coop and big shed. The whole place was peaceful and spacious, and it felt good.

We circled back to the house and stood under the balcony.

'Home sweet home?' I said to Pete, and he smiled in agreement.

We put an offer in that night. It was an unusual number, as it was all our birthday years put together – mine, Pete's, and our two daughters. It felt symbolic that we found it on Pete's birthday, and life is too short for boring, run-of-the-mill house offers.

'Even the nine cents?' the agent asked, slightly confused. He had probably never seen anything like it.

But we wrote a letter to the owners explaining the unusual number and telling them how much we loved their house, how we could see our girls enjoying the chicken coop and running in the big field and climbing the trees.

The agent reported back that the owners loved our letter and accepted our offer. We had two weeks until the offer went unconditional. Two weeks to get all our financial ducks in a row.

Fuck.

Applying for finance brought up all my stuff. With both of us self-employed, one of us in the start-up phase of business, and the other with a bad credit history, our financials were less than awesome. So we crossed everything and smiled sweetly at the impossibly young bank manager and crammed as many cherries as we possibly could on top of our application.

And then we waited for the mortgage gods to decide our fate.

In those two weeks while we waited, we threw everything at it.

I'm talking crystal grids, full moon spells, decluttering, forgiveness rituals, f-bomb affirmations, offerings to the deities of abundance, the works!

If anything had a hint of 'this might help,' I was all over it. No limiting beliefs snuck past me in this time. I examined each and every one of them and did not let them pass go.

It was an intense time. I wanted this so badly, but it was bringing up all my stories, and the fear was there, too. The house felt too good to be true; I was scared the finance would fall through. I was scared that this dream house, so close, would vanish, and I would be left with all my 'not good enough' feelings.

But I faced the fear daily and kept holding strong to the vision of the house as ours. I witnessed the fear, but I didn't let it take over.

Anytime I wavered, there was a little sign of confirmation. The 'perfect for enjoying the view' half-moon sofa that we wanted was half price, the timing of our tax return was divine, we kept seeing double rainbows, clients paid us in advance, and our bank balances were the best they had ever been.

On our second visit to the house we met the current owners, and they walked us around the garden. The owners before them had been horticulturists, and they pointed out the abundance of trees.

'There's three mango trees.'

'No way!' I remembered our London vision board.

'Yes, and two coconut palms and one banana and two avocado trees.'

I stopped. 'Two avocado trees?'

I recalled what had been on my vision board. Mango *and* avocado. My mind was just a little fucking blown, and I made a mental note to find the vision board pictures.

These trees felt like the biggest confirmation of all.

Finance was approved on my birthday.

And we moved in on the eve of our youngest daughter's birthday.

After unpacking the essentials, I set to finding the old vision board pictures, the ones of the mango and avocado trees. But when I found them, and I saw the picture of the house, too, I was shocked. I had totally forgotten what house we had on that vision board. I headed straight to the garden to compare the picture of the house to our actual house.

My mind blew open even more.

This shit clearly works.

But how?

But how the fuck *does* it actually work?

In this chapter, I'm going to show you how our thoughts can interact with and impact the world around us. We'll start with a quick summary of the law of attraction, and then we'll look at a more scientific approach to this somewhat 'woo woo' concept.

No doubt you've heard of the law of attraction. Or LOA, as the cool kids refer to it.

The law of attraction gained popularity with the book and movie *The Secret* by Rhonda Byrne. In it, Byrne explains the formula for 'getting what you want'. In short, it's 'ask, believe, and receive'. Once you're clear on what you want, you focus on it, thinking about it in positive ways and with happy feelings, and then you see yourself already having it. Then, 'hey presto', more often than not, it arrives.

Another popular LOA book is Esther Hicks's *Ask and It Is Given*. Hicks says that you get what you think about – no matter if it's good or bad – and so you must align your thoughts with what you want. Her three-step formula is a little different from Byrne's in that you 'Ask, the Universe answers and then you allow it.' Hicks focuses more on the importance of being a vibrational match to your desires; the goal is to become aligned. Once you're aligned, you can easily attract that which you desire into your life.

But the law of attraction was a thing long before it was made popular by the likes of Byrne and Hicks. In fact, *The Secret* was itself inspired by the 1910 book *The Science of Getting Rich* by Wallace D. Wattles. And Napoleon Hill's famous book *Think and Grow Rich*, published in 1937, begins with the line 'Truly "thoughts are things", and powerful things at that…'

There is something about the law of attraction that speaks to the part of us which knows our power. That feels it through and through, regardless of what our outside circumstances may tell us. This is a deep knowledge of and belief in *ourselves* and our *access to possibility*. However, it is so deep that it has become muffled by voices of our culture that benefit from telling us otherwise. There will be more about these voices and how to tell them to 'eff off' in Chapters 6 and 7.

While I may have one foot in woo-woo land, the other is firmly rooted in logic and science. I like me some proof. And not proof of the 'it worked for me' kind, but proof of the 'here's the science to explain why the fuck this happens' kind.

I wanted something to back up these claims by the LOA experts. I wanted something a bit meatier, something a bit more science-based, something to convince myself that this isn't just a coincidence.

The convincer came when I read about an amazing experiment in Dr Joe Dispenza's epic book, *Becoming Supernatural.*

French researcher Rene Peoc'h allowed baby chickens to bond with and imprint on a robot. Imprinting is a biological function crucial for a newborn chick's survival. Once they bond with their mother, they will follow her and desire to be near her, thus increasing their chances of surviving.

This adoptive mother robot had been programmed to randomly walk in all directions via a random number generator. When left to its own devices, it did indeed walk randomly.

However, and this is when it gets interesting, once the chickens were placed behind a glass partition in the same area as the robot, this mama's 'random' movements became not so random. In fact, the robot spent a significant amount of time closest to the baby chicks.

These chicks affected the movement of a randomly programmed robot.

Yep, let's say that again.

The 'yearning' of the chicks affected the movement of a randomly programmed robot.

Similar studies have been done on humans affecting random number generators. Dunne and her team at the Princeton Engineering Anomalies Research Laboratory had subjects affect the random number generators by asking them to focus on either higher or lower numbers. They found two-thirds of people were able to influence the machine to create higher or lower numbers when asked. And, interestingly, the effects were greater when two people with an emotional attachment worked together.

What this means is our thoughts and feelings **can** affect the world around us.

And that effect is greater when there is some emotional connection, such as a drive to bond like the chicks or a pre-established loving relationship.

There is something at play here, some kind of unseen interaction between the cells that fill our skin suits and the things outside of these suits.

How is this possible?

Perhaps in 50 years' time this will be a very common, easily accepted, widely used and understood concept. Perhaps like the theory of germs, this will be quite simply explained once science catches up. Perhaps my grandchildren's generation will be the ones to figure out how this actually works.

For now, let's just accept that something pretty magic is going on.

Except when it doesn't. Because, crazy complicated creatures that we are, we tend to get in our own way.

We don't realise the power of our thoughts and our agency in our interactions with the world. Like the chicks just doing their thing, we merely go about our daily lives following the neural impulses of our biology, not realising that it is our very impulses co-creating the world with which we engage on a daily basis.

Perhaps we could think of it like an unseen conversation.

Sitting in the corner of the pub here, struggling to write, because I have left it too late to be a real writer. The book, this rambling outpouring of beer-

fogged musings that I'm embarrassed to call a book, won't be interesting to anyone else.

Or

Sitting in the corner of the pub here, creating my book, the book that soon people will be reading in pubs themselves, the book that will fuel beer-fogged conversations and mind-blowing musings, the book that will effing change lives!

These thought processes put out very different energy. If it were a conversation with the world, the world might reply to the first:

'Ah, okay, struggle. She wants struggle. Also, this is too late for her, make sure we match that. Oh, it's just some musings, and she doesn't want it to interest others.'

To the second one:

'Ah, a book. It's a book, a real book she's writing. Many others will read it, and it will inspire conversations and change lives!'

Once we understand that our thoughts, desires, and drives can in fact impact the world around us... Well, this is where the magic begins. This is where we can use our complicated bits, aka our brains, and have them to work in our favour. If we harness the immense power of our minds and our biology, we can literally change our world.

We've looked at how the brain gathers information about our world, and how that information is then saved and used to inform our experience and perception of the world. But knowing that our brains can also have a direct effect on the world around us, that we can influence the physical environment – say what?! Well, that changes the playing field, doesn't it?

Yes, our thoughts and our emotions, like the chicks, are effing powerful. Powerful enough that we can change not only our biology, but also potentially the world around us, too.

In the next chapter, we will look at what we can use to bridge the gap between our *feeling* and *thinking* brains, and how we can get them working together.

Too Long; Didn't Read

- Your thoughts become things.
- Your thoughts can influence the world around you.
- The world responds to your thoughts.
- When you understand this, you can literally change your world.

4
CREATING A BRIDGE BETWEEN YOUR *FEELING* BRAIN AND YOUR *THINKING* BRAIN

The leather seat is deliciously soft beneath me. I look out my window, catching someone smiling at me and then nodding at my car, as if to say, 'Cheers, well done you.' I beam back and pinch myself as I recall what I am in fact driving.

A Tesla.

I'm driving a fucking Tesla!

The latest SUV model, with voice-activated controls and leather interior.

Yep, this is my life now.

I breathe in this feeling. It feels abundant and light. It feels like a true expression of my potential. And it feels so normal.

I guess it *is* my new normal now.

The light turns green and my grin widens as I silently accelerate.

But the grin is slapped from my face by my toddler, who must have found her way into my bed sometime last night. I groggily open my eyes, and as the smell of the leather interior fades away, I meet my daughter's cheeky gaze two inches from my face.

I smile at her, but am soon greeted with quite another morning smell.

'I poo, Mama.'

Ah, the Tesla will have to wait; the joys of motherhood are more pressing right now.

As I wipe my daughter's poo from her legs – noting for the umpteenth time that corn doesn't seem to digest – I start thinking about the Tesla and why it has to wait.

I ask myself: why not?

Why can't I have a Tesla?

Why can't I, NatalieMotherFuckingQueen ManifestorStokell, have a Tesla?

Between wipes, the answers come tumbling out, tripping over themselves before I can censor them:

I can't afford it...

How will I afford it?

I'm not that kind of person...

After securing a new nappy on a now clean human alarm clock, I wash my hands. Then I look at myself in the mirror and start a conversation.

It goes something like this:

Mirror Self:

What do you mean, 'not that kind of person'?

Me:

You know, the kind of person who drives a Tesla!

Mirror Self:

What kind of person drives a Tesla?

Me:

Um, well, they have perfectly blow-dried hair and salon-manicured nails.

Mirror Self:

Hang on, this is familiar. This sounds like one of those Turkish expats in Istanbul.

Me:

Yes! They would totally drive a Tesla!

Mirror Self:

Okay, so talk a little more about these women.

Me:

Um, well I certainly don't want to be one, have you seen my nails?! [I hold them up to the mirror in all their unmanicured glory, hoping that it's just dirt and not poo under my index finger.]

Mirror Self:

Okay, so if you don't want to be one of these women, and these are the kind of women who drive a Tesla... Then what does that mean about the possibility of you driving a Tesla?

Me:

Oh. So...? I should get my nails done, and then the possibility of me driving a Tesla will open up...? What the actual fuck?!

Mirror Self:

No, come on, honey, use that juicy walnut in your head now. Let's break that one down.

Me:

Okay. How am I going to be driving a Tesla if I believe that only people who have salon nails are allowed to drive Teslas?!

Mirror Self:

Yes! So, there's a link here between something you want – a Tesla – and something you don't want – salon nails.

Me:

This sounds kinda fucked up, right?

Mirror Self:

Hmmm, well, let's just ask if it is helpful or unhelpful. Does this association serve us?

Me:

Hell no! This is one of those batshit crazy kinds of limiting beliefs, isn't it!

Mirror Self:

It sure is, honey. Now, what are we going to do about it?!

Later that afternoon, in that blessed hour of nap time, I sat down with my journal. I let my pen explore these limiting beliefs and all the reasons why I couldn't have a Tesla further.

As I wrote and wrote I unpeeled layers of beliefs, and I started to see some themes. After three pages, I finally got to what felt like the root of the issue:

Not feeling good enough.

Ah, feck, that ole chestnut.

But at least I got there.

Only when I reached this root belief was I able to start replacing those 'batshit crazy' beliefs with much more helpful and empowering ones. Ones that were much more likely to result in me being a Tesla owner.

Ones like:

'I am enough.'

'I am worthy and enough just as I am.'

'I am perfectly worthy right here and right now.'

I might not have my Tesla yet, but it feels much closer and more within my reach. The belief that I can be a Tesla owner sits more easily now; it rests on me like a cosy T-shirt rather than a starched beige blouse. It's more *me*.

In the previous chapters, we looked at how the brain works to form beliefs and how our brains can affect the world around us. Now it's time to start thinking about how we can change our beliefs so we can affect the world around us in ways that aren't 'fucked up.' Or, as my mirror self says, how can we affect the world in ways that are 'helpful' as opposed to 'unhelpful'?

In this chapter, I'm going to introduce you to the idea that language is the key to connecting your *feeling* brain with your *thinking* brain. Then we will uncover some of your heart's desires and get ready to dive into the second part of the book – the part where you invite more awesome into your life.

★

Unlike those darling baby chickens in the last chapter, we are lucky enough to have a very developed *thinking* brain. A big part of what distinguishes us from animals is our advanced ability to use this part of our brain.

And the main way we use our *thinking* brain is with language.

We use language both *externally,* with verbal expression to communicate, and also *internally,* in our cognitive processing as we make sense of the world.

Language can be seen as a vital link or bridge between our *feeling* and our *thinking* brains.

When we are young, and before we become verbal, many of our memories are stored in ways that we can't access with our *thinking* brain. Instead, the emotional states are recorded and stored as feelings, maybe even as a smell or a taste; they're vague and can be hard to pinpoint. We might smell a fragrance that someone from our early childhood used to wear, and a feeling arises rather than recollection of a specific memory.

Because we didn't have the *language* to create the memory, the memory is stored as a *feeling*. It's only when we become verbal that language gives us something to structure and to 'hook' our memories around. Language allows us to make more cognitive sense of the world. It enables us to give meaning to all the things we previously experienced merely as a bundle of feelings.

Language Is One of the Most Powerful Tools in Our Arsenal

Not only does language provide a bridge between our *thinking* and *feeling* brains, but it can also be a tool to get our *feeling* and *thinking* brains working together.

And if we can get these two to work together, we can move beyond the evolutionary purpose of surviving and into the soul purpose of thriving.

How Can We Use Language in a Simple and Effective Way?

Let's look at language like commands for a computer. If language is the commands, our brain is the computer, merely obeying the commands. If the brain is the hardware or the computer, then our thoughts are the software or the program running on that computer.

Stop for a minute now and become aware of the thoughts that have been preoccupying your mind today. What programs are you running? And what programs could you be running instead?

Sometimes our programs are so ingrained it takes a lot of navel gazing to see them.

6am

I wake to an empty bed. The sun streams in through the slats in the blinds. The bed is empty. I wonder where Pete is. I wonder *how* Pete is.

How is he feeling? Is he having a low day? Or a high one?

He's just come back from a month in Peru. A child-free, work-free, girlfriend-free month of sacred sites and circles with shamans in Peru.

Is he adjusting okay? Does he wish he wasn't here?

My journal beckons, but I ignore it. I am battling the desire to forgo my morning writing ritual and find Pete instead.

Don't do it, Natalie. He's okay. You don't need to know how he is.

Ignoring this voice, I throw back the covers and leave the room in search of Pete.

I find him in the kitchen, making breakfast. He looks up when he hears me come in and I scan his face for clues.

Is that a frown? Are his eyes soft or hard? Is his mouth heavy with sadness?

Fuck, I'm doing it again!

Hypervigilance is a program I've only recently become aware that I'm running. And fark, is it hard to shift. The neural patterns are strong, the pathways thick and deeply ingrained.

When I was a child, these patterns served me. I needed to be hyperaware of how my mother was feeling. Was she in a low patch? Would I have to tiptoe around and be careful?

But now, as an adult, that feeling was hard to shake. It felt natural. It felt normal. But it was causing me anxiety, and it didn't feel like a healthy way of relating to my partner. Becoming aware of this program was the first step in changing it.

How Do We Change a Program?

Well, let's go back to the computer analogy. To change a computer program, we just give it new commands.

And what is the human equivalent of writing new commands?

Language.

We speak to it.

And an awesome way to give it new commands is, quite simply, with affirmations.

'Tous les jours à tous points de vue je vais de mieux en mieux'

French apothecarist Émile Coué was one of the earliest adopters of affirmations. After graduating pharmacology in 1876, Coué started noting that the more he praised a medication to his patients, the more effective the medication was. He began to explore this further and looked firstly into hypnosis and then auto-suggestion. He was a big proponent of people curing themselves and saw his role as facilitating this process rather than healing. Eventually he left the apothecary and developed his own method, called the Coue Method. This incorporated elements of hypnosis and self-hypnosis, imagination, and positive thinking. But he is most famous for the affirmation he requested his patients repeat multiple times a day:

'Every day in every way I am getting better and better.'

Today it is one of my favourite affirmations – of course, I add my own flavour to it, as you will find out in Chapter 9.

So, essentially, you have all you need to know. You understand the way beliefs are formed and you understand the effect your thoughts and desires can have on the world around you. And you know that language is the key to changing the unhelpful beliefs and programs that you have been running.

You can use language – in the form of affirmations – to create a bridge between your *thinking* brain and your *feeling* brain, between your thoughts and your feelings. Language is the tool to get our *feeling* brain on board with our *thinking* brain.

Just say your affirmations, folks!

Is That It?!

But why the fuck don't they always work?

Why are they so simple, but so hit and miss?

Why do some resonate like crazy, and others feel ho-hum?

Million-dollar questions.

And lucky you, you're holding a book which contains the answers.

Our *feeling* brain is older than our *thinking* brain. Our *feeling* brain is backed up by years of evolution and subsequently could be seen as more dominant than the *thinking* parts of our brain.

But if you can harness the evolution-backed power of your *feeling* brain and the cognitive power of your *thinking* brain, this is where the true power lies.

In Part Two of this book, I will show you five hacks. These hacks will help you to use the power of your brain to your advantage. Rather than being a slave to your brain, you will make it work for you. These hacks will help you harness the stellar power of that giant juicy walnut you have inside your head.

Each of these are affirmation hacks. They will use the power of your brain to make your affirmations even more powerful and effective - to supercharge them, if you like.

These affirmation hacks will also help you to uncover those sneaky, limiting beliefs that are not working in your favour. These sneaky limiting beliefs, or SLBs, are a big part of what stops our affirmations from working.

In order for your affirmations to work, before you can change the show, there must be cognitive awareness of what beliefs are running the show. Then you can work with the power of the *feeling* brain.

Each chapter will end with some invitations for you to dive deeper and explore. This diving is where the magic happens. It is all very well reading about things which can change your life. It is quite another actually taking action. So, I encourage you to do the exercises.

Do. The. Fucking. Exercises.

I've made a workbook for those of you motivated by that kind of thing. Download it and print, get some new sparkly pens and fill it in as you go: www.fbombaffirmations/book/workbook

But first, we must think of some of our dreams, desires, and goals. Then we can frame this work around them and really get some magic happening!

What Do You Want to Be, Do, and Have?

Writing your 'be, do, and have' lists are a great way to come up with some goals and desires.

Grab a pen and paper and start brainstorming the ends to these statements:

Things I want to be...

Things I want to have...

Things I want to do...

I want to be...socially confident...an Instagram influencer...a boutique gin maker...comfortable in my skin...healthy AF...flexible enough to do the splits...

I want to have...a Tesla...a pair of perfect-for-me jeans...a weekly cleaner...a personal chef...inner peace...

I want...to make enough passive income to replace my salary...to travel to Italy...to live a year in Europe...to learn guitar...to finish my degree...to travel to an island with my bestie...

Freewrite and really give yourself permission to dream. Fill a page at least. And then another page. Don't censor yourself. If it feels hard, just pretend. Go to that space where 8-year-old you lives, and daydream.

Then read over the list and pick three. One that feels doable, one that feels like a stretch, and one that feels an impossibility.

These three are the ones we will work with for the rest of the book.

Too Long; Didn't Read

- Language is the perfect bridge between your *feeling* brain and your *thinking* brain.
- Affirmations are a simple but not always effective way to use language.
- Affirmations aren't always effective because we need to be aware of the underlying programs or sneaky limiting beliefs (SLBs) that we have wired in our brains.

- Once we are aware of our SLBs, then we can change them.
- I'm going to introduce you in the next part of the book to five affirmation hacks.
- Do the exercises at the end of each chapter – the doing is where the magic happens!

PART TWO

5
'IT IS SAFE...'

The sun is that perfect temperature of a Queensland winter, and as it warms my bikini-clad skin, my body softens and relaxes.

I'm sitting on a towel at the edge of the pool at our local swim centre. It's quiet, and my girls have the pool to themselves. I watch them play and I go over the week ahead and my mental to-do list.

Tweak the new affirmation tracks...pay the rates...the morning meeting at school...the emails awaiting a reply...

Then I recall the promise I made to my coach – the three promises, in fact:

One, I would do the damn website.

Two, I would record a letter to my SoundCloud subscribers.

Three, I would finish my launch timeline.

Fark. Why did I promise these things?

I'm not ready.

Just the thought of these actions makes my stomach clench. I feel like a deer in headlights. Frozen. Not knowing which way to turn.

What if I can't do the tech side?

What if I launch it, and people don't like it?

What if I launch to crickets?

The overwhelm starts to kick in and I can feel the buzz of adrenaline in my body. My leg starts to twitch, as if impatient, as if I want to get up and run.

Oh, fuck.

This is too big. I don't think I can do this.

I don't know if it will succeed.

What if it flops?

What if it flies?

What if I can't keep up with demand?

What if it goes viral and I get hate mail?

As the thoughts gather momentum, I can feel the buzz of adrenaline get louder in my body. I really want to launch, but I'm also in so much fear over it. I'm scared by all the possibilities and potentials. Even the good ones – the ones where it goes viral in the best possible way – feel overwhelming, and it's too much. It's like my head is going into overload and I can't cope.

Ah, shite, I can't handle this.

My leg bounces up and down faster and my stomach knots itself further. I rub my temples to ward off the headache I can feel creeping in.

There is a splash and a cry from the pool.

'Mama! Mama! She hit me!'

'WHAT?!' I turn to glare at them. They look at me with wide eyes, confused at my uncharacteristic anger. I instantly regret my outburst. 'Oh, I'm sorry, my loves, I'm just feeling stressed. Come here, let's have a hug.'

As their wet little bodies lean into mine, I breathe deeply and try to calm myself.

Maybe I'll leave it. The website can wait until next week, or maybe next month. There's no real rush.

I take some more deep, slow breaths.

And I feel both relieved and disappointed in myself.

Let's return to what we learnt in previous chapters to dissect what just happened.

What's actually going on here is that the brain is just 'doing its thang' – gathering information about the world – and has registered a threat. But not an outside threat. Instead, it's picked up on an internal threat, a threat in the form of thoughts.

Remember, the brain doesn't know the difference between something that's really happening and something we imagine is happening.

Either way, it is information that the brain perceives as a threat: 'This isn't safe!'

And when something registers as unsafe, we don't go there. In fact, we often run as far as we can in the opposite direction. This response has been called the 'fight or flight' response, where in response to the perceived threat we prepare either to fight it or to flee from it.

From an evolutionary perspective, this a wonderful, wonderful response, one that has enabled humans to survive attacks by sabre tooth tigers and the like. Once this response is triggered, it optimises our ability to physically respond to a situation. It takes oxygen from the parts of the body that don't need it for fighting or fleeing, such as our brain and our digestive and reproductive systems, and it sends oxygen to the parts that do, such as our muscular and circulatory systems.

When a threat is perceived by the brain, a physiological chain reaction is set off in our bodies. It's like our brains yell out:

'Move away from the unsafe thing. Initiate "Respond to a threat protocol".'

And the body replies:

'Muscular system engaged and ready to move quickly.

'Reproductive system disengaged.

'Digestive system disengaged.

'Circulatory system engaged.

'We are ready to get the hell away from this threat – let's go!'

This is an awesome response to a perceived fear, if the threat is a temporary one. However, it becomes problematic when the threat is ongoing, when it's not something that we can run away from.

When we are faced with an ongoing, everyday stressor – like an overbearing boss, not enough money and too much month left, noisy neighbours who keep ungodly hours, or an unhelpful belief – our body still initiates the 'respond to threat' protocol. These stressors are the modern-day sabre tooth tigers. Our brain doesn't distinguish between different threats. It just knows there is one.

If the response to a threat is to pull blood containing oxygen and nutrients away from the organs, then what could be the effect of this long term? It's no coincidence that in this day and age we seem to have an increase of fertility and digestive issues, heart problems, muscular tension, high blood pressure, and immune-related illnesses.

While it's a well-known fact that stress is the cause of 80% of illnesses, what people need to understand is that this is just our inbuilt response. It's one that serves us very well when the threat is temporary. When the threat is ongoing – this is where it becomes problematic.

How Do Our Beliefs Come Into Play as Threats?

Think of a goal. A big, scary, kinda out there, 'I can't tell that judgey friend' kind of goal.

Yep, you know the one – the goal, not the judgey friend.

No doubt there's something about this goal that scares you.

Let's return back to that experience by the pool.

When I got home that day, and once the girls were in bed, I grabbed my journal and started to delve into why I didn't want to launch. I realised that I wasn't afraid of not mastering the tech, or of all the things a launch involved.

It was instead the fear of becoming visible. The fear of exposing myself to rejection, ridicule, or judgement.

This is what felt unsafe and threatening to my survival. My brain didn't register it any differently from a physical threat in my environment, such as someone or something attacking me. My brain just knows 'ah, rejection from the group, this isn't safe; we need to stay together to survive.' This is the power of biology.

To my brain, a predator, a scary boss, or the thought of being visible were all the same – they all produced the same physiological and biochemical response in my body. In this moment for me, the urge to run was manifesting in my restless leg twitching. I needed to expel some of the built-up adrenaline, and I also needed to complete the stress cycle. When this cycle doesn't complete, we can stay stuck in the same spot, in the same place of 'ready to run'. I was on alert and quick to respond with anger when my girls called out. And I was finding it hard to slow down and organise my thoughts.

So, how can we reassure ourselves that these unhelpful beliefs and thoughts are not in fact predators coming to attack us? Could we use our *thinking* brain to overpower our *feeling* brain?

And what happens when we do?

I'm going to take you back to my favourite decade to find out: the decade that brought us the *Fresh Prince of Bel Air,* the Clinton BJ, and the Walkman. The '90s.

I looked down at the white wash of the rushing river 134 metres below.

Fuck.

Don't look down.

I returned my gaze to the horizon and swallowed the lump in my throat, the beginning of rising nausea.

134 fucking metres to the bottom. This was ridiculous.

What the fuck am I doing?

Just do it. Don't think.

I turned and smiled at the camera, and then, arms out, I pushed off the platform and dove out as far as I could.

As the water raced towards me, my head freaked the fuck out. It was like the program running in my brain glitched. The most dominant thought was this:

'What the fuck have you done?! You are going to die! You don't want to die!'

I was stunned into silence as the water got closer and closer. If my dominant thought was survival, my dominant feeling was confusion.

What the fuck had I done?

It was like I was unable to comprehend that I'd put myself in a situation that, to my *feeling* brain, felt like a 0% chance of survival.

Then, right when the water was at my fingertips, the cord jerked and I was rebounding back up.

My *feeling* brain caught up with my *thinking* brain:

Oh, what? We survived? Halle-fucking-louya, we're alive!

Champagne lids were popped off endorphins, and the adrenaline rush of relief flooded my veins. I had bungee-jumped off the tallest bridge in New Zealand!

I was still shocked into silence, but I was grinning madly when the bouncing stopped and the boat pulled in to retrieve me. And as I walked up 134 metres of steps, adrenaline and endorphins pumped through my veins like some of the best class A's I'd ever had.

If I had let my *feeling* brain take over, I wouldn't have experienced that adrenaline rush. I would have stayed in fear. But instead, I allowed my *thinking* brain to lead the way, and the payoff was the feeling of satisfaction and the boost in confidence.

Actually, this is a great exercise when you are at a crossroads, stalled in fear with which way to turn. By doing something you're scared of, you are proving to yourself that you are capable of overcoming your fears. It might not be jumping off a bridge or out of a plane. It could just be a small thing, like making a phone call or doing something out of your comfort zone.

Just outside of your comfort zone is where the growth happens.

And it is growth in the true sense of the word. By doing something new, you literally grow new neural networks in your brain.

Courage comes from the Latin *cor*, meaning *heart*. It is defined as 'the ability to control your fear in a dangerous or difficult situation.'

Courage is a very human attribute and one of the best antidotes to fear.

The biochemical payoff of pushing through fear is pretty epic. The adrenaline rush and the endorphins of survival are strong enough that when you've experienced them once, you'll want to feel them again. This is evolution's way of ensuring that we do in fact push through and survive.

More About the Stress Cycle

Like many processes in our body, the stress response is a cycle:

> Perceived threat registered by your brain: 'Help! I'm not safe!' → your body reacts physiologically to prepare to respond to the threat → your brain responds cognitively → informed by your brain, your behaviour adapts to deal with the threat → threat is gone: 'Hooray! I'm safe.'

This is all very well when the threat is a sabre tooth tiger nearby, or an in-law staying at your house, and we can escape or count down the days until they leave. The cycle is able to complete, and at the end, we're able to feel that elation that we're now safe.

But can you see where you could get stuck in this cycle when the stress is chronic? Or when it's an internal 'threatening' thought that you keep thinking? There is no resolution, and the cycle can't complete.

Sometimes when a thought causes us an immense amount of stress, we need to help our body complete the cycle. We will not be able to engage with the thought cognitively until we have engaged with it physiologically. We need to work in ways that our feeling brain understands before we can work with our thinking brain.

While we may not be able to escape the thought, before we change it, we need to allow it to feel part of a complete cycle:

I closed my journal.

Fear of visibility. WTF?!

I don't need that.

I gotta shift this one.

I grabbed my headphones and found one of my favourite body-moving playlists. I turned it up loud so my head would be full of the music. So full that any thoughts wouldn't have room in there, too.

Taking a deep breath, I tuned into that feeling of fear.

Goodbye fear.

You have served your purpose, but I don't need you no more!

Then I pressed play.

The beat was strong and I started to move my body to its pace. The tempo picked up. And I took a few deep breaths as I moved faster to match the speed of the music. I was quickly lost in it. Moving swiftly, I allowed my body to release any tension from the thoughts that had arisen after journaling. And soon I was feeling endorphins tingle under my skin, endorphins not dissimilar to those I might feel if I had in fact escaped the threat.

After I journaled and found the root of the fear, I knew I needed to do something to allow the cycle to complete before I started changing my thoughts around it. Dance is a great release for me. Any physical movement or physiological process can help, though – go for a run or have a horizontal dance with someone who has been giving you the glad-eye.

Another simple way to release tension is to let yourself have a cry.

Tears Are the Safety Valve of the Heart

I set up a blanket on the grass and placed the tray of food and drink to one side of it, a small pile of books on the other. I lay down on the blanket and took some deep breaths. And I tried not to think of the events of the day before.

The sounds she made as she was being attacked, though!

It's over. She's okay.

Deep breaths. I looked to the field and could see that she was okay. She was sitting, but she had been up and back to grazing today. Yesterday she didn't eat a thing. Nor did I.

Her eyes wide, looking at me as she shakily stood, blood dripping from her long neck.

It was like a live David Attenborough in our backyard. The two dogs – wolf- or lion-like in their chase – the alpacas – deer-like, running for their lives.

The tears start to well. I let them fall.

It's okay. She's okay. I'm okay.

And that's how I spent the day, crying, resting, reading. All of it punctuated by long gazes at our three alpacas, gazes filled with relief. Relief that the attack hadn't been fatal. Relief that I had been home and heard her cries. Relief that our neighbour was able to get her dogs off in time.

★

When your darling brain just 'does its thang,' i.e. prepares to fight or flee, and your sweet body just responds to that, i.e. prepares to fight or flee, sometimes you need to work with it in ways that it understands.

Witnessing our alpacas, who feel like part of the family, being attacked triggered a huge stress response in me. My adrenalin was firing through my body, and I went straight into 'fight' mode. I grabbed the baseball bat and ran to the end of the field, yelling a wordless war cry like some warrior going to battle. But after, once the neighbour had left, tail between her legs like her dogs, and the threat had gone, I was still shaky and on edge. That day I did all the things that needed doing, calling vets until I found one that was free to come and check her, gently herding her into the holding pen, holding space for her. But I felt stuck in stress. That night I couldn't sleep; I was on edge and jumpy at any noise. The next day I knew I needed to help my body switch back into 'rest and repose.'

In these busy times we find ourselves in today, we have begun to overlook the importance of rest. Rest is actually an important and physiologically necessary process, one needed to help our body recover and repair from the wear and tear of daily life. Rest is not being lazy or 'checking out.' Rest is vital for our good health.

And sometimes we need help to switch out of the stress response and into the rest response. If you find yourself stuck in a stress cycle, you can use your physiology to 'hack' and shift from the cycle. This hacking can disrupt the cycle, which then allows it to complete.

- Breathing is deceptively simple, and only in recent years have I truly understood its power.

Slow, deep breaths send the message to our brains that we are relaxed; they're like an off switch for your sympathetic nervous system and an on switch for your parasympathetic nervous system.

- Lying down tells the body to rest; it engages the parasympathetic nervous system.
- Crying is also a clever way to relieve stress. Research has shown that tears contain stress hormones, so you are literally letting go of stress as you cry.
- Physical movement, like aerobic exercise or dancing, not only reduces stress hormones but creates endorphins, too.

Our big goals and desires can trigger our fears. You may need to do something to physically move through and complete the stress cycle before you can change your thoughts around them.

How Do We Apply This to Our Dreams, Intentions, and Affirmations?

If our goals and desires trigger an internal fear response, then we will not have our brain and its power on our side in their manifesting. Rather than attracting them to us, we will repel them.

Our *thinking* brain might be all 'I want to have a multiple six-figure business,' but if we have some beliefs around what that means, i.e. visibility beliefs, then our *feeling* brain will be all 'um, I don't think so!'

Our *feeling* brain senses the threat. Our *feeling* brain does not want this to happen, and it responds by immediately initiating the 'respond to threat' protocol.

In the last chapter, we spoke about language as a bridge between the two brains. Let's create a bridge.

'It Is Safe for Me To...'

Very simply, by adding 'It is safe for me to...' to the front of your goals, you create a beautiful bridge, a calming 'Japanese garden with tinkling water beneath it' kind of bridge. A bridge between your *thinking* brain and your *feeling* brain. By doing this, you consciously use language to combat any fear triggering the stress response.

By adding this to the front of your goal, you create a powerful affirmation that utilises the power of both your *feeling* and *thinking* brains.

Try it: pick one of your big goals and add 'It is safe for me to...' in front of it.

These six small words create a sense of courage, a reminder that we can in fact do this – that we have, in fact, got this.

Part of the process of challenging our fears is understanding where they are coming from. You may find that it's some SLBs that trigger the fears. Take some time to go through the exercises below and see what you uncover.

Your Turn

Go back to the desires and goals you came up with in the last chapter and add 'It is safe for me to' in front of them. In doing this, you are reassuring yourself that it is safe to have this desire.

How does that feel?

You may also be surprised at what thoughts come up when you tell yourself this. It may be revealed that it actually doesn't feel very safe. And you may not have realised how 'not safe' this actually feels.

Adding these words shines a light on and brings to the surface our true feelings about how it could be to actually have this desire. These words will help to reveal some of those SLBs that are actually blocking you from these desires.

Play With It

Grab a pen and paper and try adding 'It is not safe for me to...because' and see what comes up.

Don't censor as you write; just allow the thoughts to flow and see what limiting beliefs rear their not so pretty heads.

Again, you may be surprised, and what comes up will give you great material for some conscious journaling.

Get Curious

Curiosity is a wonderful mindset to embrace when working with these limiting beliefs. When we get curious, we are a little detached as well as a little elevated above the intensity of any feelings.

Curiosity elevates us from the magnetic pull of the feeling and places us into the *thoughts* about the feeling.

Essentially, curiosity takes us from the *feeling* brain and engages the *thinking* brain. It can be a wonderful circuit breaker.

When we are curious, we are investigative and questioning. How a question is asked can actually be just as important as the content of the question.

Asking a question in a particular way will set up how we think about the answer.

Asking 'how' questions is a great way to tap into the energy of curiosity. 'How' questions are often more helpful than 'why' questions.

Compare 'how can I shift this?' to 'why can't I shift this?' One keeps us in the negative, keeps us in the feeling, while the other allows us to move out of it.

Try playing with different questions around your fears. Freewrite and see what comes up.

How can I drop the fear around this?

What do I need to do to let go of this fear?

Who would I be if I wasn't scared of this?

The way we frame a question will inform the answer.

What Comes Up?

Are there any themes to the limiting beliefs that come up?

Are any memories triggered from these themes?

Can you journal a little deeper and see if you can reach the origin story?

Imagine **

Lie down somewhere super comfy and 'safe' for you. This might be your bed or your favourite spot on your sofa. Close your eyes and take some slow, deep breaths.

When you feel your body start to soften into a more relaxed state, imagine and see in your mind's eye a small, pearl-like golden light around your heart. As you breathe, start to see this slowly expand and grow. As it grows and moves through your body, every cell is covered in this golden light. And you start to realise it is like a forcefield, a protective light of safety. You breathe deeply and it gently expands until it completely encases your whole body. You have a shimmery golden bubble around you, your own forcefield keeping you safe.

Think of some things in your life which make you feel safe and invite them into the bubble with you. They might be your favourite pet, or your favourite human, your best crystal, that cosy blanket on your bed... Create a cosy den of comfort and safety.

As you rest inside this bubble, you feel deeply relaxed and completely safe.

When you are ready, gently allow the bubble to shrink back to marble sized and see it safe and snug in your heart space. It is always here for you; you simply need to take some deep breaths to activate it and bring it back to a complete forcefield around your body.

Hack It Daily

Circuit breakers are effective for all unhelpful thoughts, but especially so for fear-based ones. Fear-based thoughts and limiting beliefs trigger a physiological response in the body, so doing something physical can interrupt and eventually disrupt this thought pattern.

- Keep a rubber band around your wrist. When you notice a fear-based belief, snap the band and tell yourself that it is safe for you.
- Or clap your hands above your head – the physical and sudden movement can help to break the cycle of fearful thoughts long enough to allow more helpful thoughts in. It's a bit like a wake-up call or slap in the face for your brain.

- Run your hands under cold water or take a cold shower. This works in the same way to break the cycle as above. In addition, the physical sensation of coldness disrupts your unhelpful thought patterns.
- Get up and move to another location – the change of scene gives your brain something new to focus on.
- Do something physical to change up your physiology and then get your thinking brain in on the action with an affirmation, beginning with 'It is safe for me to…'

Make up your favourite acronym for fear. You've probably heard False Evidence Appearing Real. I like:

Fuck Everything And Remember

As in, remember that it's just your beautiful feeling brain.

Or:

Feelings Everywhere Aren't Reality

They're just your *feeling* brain doing its 'thang'.

Do something that scares you. It can be something little, like making a phone call or emailing a mentor, or you could go big and jump out of a plane.

Too Long; Didn't Read

- Sometimes our thoughts can be perceived as a threat by our brain.
- Our brain wants to escape threats.
- If we have goals that scare us too much or trigger thoughts about ourselves that don't feel safe, then we may trigger a stress response in our body.

- Until we complete that cycle, it may be hard to reach that goal.
- You can help your body to complete a stress cycle using your physiology, e.g. breath, movement, tears.
- Once the cycle is complete, you can engage cognitively.
- Use the words 'It is safe for me to...' in front of your affirmations to reassure yourself.
- Use the words 'It is not safe for me to...' to find out any sneaky limiting beliefs.

** All the 'imagines' in Part Two of the book are pre-recorded for you. Simply visit

www.fbombaffirmations/book/imagine

6
'I AM ALLOWED...'

The bass is heavy.

I can feel it vibrate through my body.

As I move with the beat, my sequin bodysuit catches and sparkles in the fairy lights strung in the trees above.

And I smile at the dancers around me.

Yes! It feels so freaking good to be dancing in nature!

I throw my head up and look at the vast expanse of stars above, and at the same time I feel my connection to the earth, to the soft grass beneath my bare feet. I feel like I am plugging in to Mother Nature.

Fuck, I needed this! I'm so glad we eventually found this place.

We had spent over an hour driving through country lanes on the outskirts of Dunedin, looking for signs of the rave we had heard about somewhat cryptically on the student radio station. Finally, we found a collection of student-like cars parked by a farm gate, and when we stopped and wound down our windows, we could hear the bass through the trees.

We followed the path to a clearing, where generators had been set up to run the speakers and decks. Fairy lights were strung through the trees, and there was a small crowd of people dancing.

This is just what I need right now.

The tempo quickens.

The energy in the crowd builds.

I move faster. My eyes remain just open enough to soft focus on the people around me so I'm aware of the spaces between us.

The music gets louder as a group of dread-headed drummers pick up their bongos and join in the beat. Feeling the live music against the electronic beats lifts my energy; a champagne bubble of joy rises in my body and I dance harder.

Yes. Yes. Yes!

People around me are smiling and losing themselves in the tribal beats.

The tune peaks and so do I. My hair flies, sequins flash, and my feet are a blur. My cheeks hurt from grinning.

I am existing completely in this moment.

Every cell in my body tingles with aliveness as I let go of the daily tension of holding on, holding in, measuring up.

Suddenly, the generator stops, and with it the music and lights are gone. But the bongos keep the beat, and with barely a moment's hesitation, everyone keeps moving to it.

Then, from the edge, a half-naked man starts yelling. He is yelling, like he's making an announcement. It's only as he gets closer that I can make out his words:

'This is not a rehearsal!' He moves across the middle of the crowd. 'This is not a rehearsal! You can be who you want to be!'

He looks like he's on a substance of the mind-altering kind, but damn, his words make sense.

This *wasn't* a fucking rehearsal. And I *could be* who I wanted to be.

It was my second year at Uni, I was coming out of what I would later realise was a spell of depression and I was in the midst of 'finding myself'. The transition from leaving home – with its ill mother and three younger brothers I was often responsible for – and being thrown into the first year shenanigans of drinking in excess, bed hopping, and navigating social pressures while also trying to study, was quite an adjustment. And in this second year, although I felt more settled, I was still finding my way.

For a few months I'd felt myself drifting from my friend group, and while I was the one initiating this, it also felt like a rejection of sorts. Perhaps I wanted my friends to notice me drifting away and to stop it? I also really wanted to let my freak flag fly, but I hadn't found my people to fly it with yet.

So here under the stars, with the half-naked man's instructions, I began to feel free.

People started cheering and woohooing, as if affirming his words. I threw my head back and looked at the stars again. I felt his words ricocheting around my being.

And I started cheering and woohooing myself.

Then the music and lights came back, and everyone clapped and the dancing resumed its intensity.

This is not a rehearsal.

I can *be who I want to be.*

Mind altering substances or not, this dude knew what he was talking about.

And I wanted in on that.

The dance floor has always been a place of freedom for me. I am lucky enough – well, some might say old enough – to have caught the end of the rave culture of the '90s.

One pro of having an ill mother and emotionally absent father was that I was often left to my own devices. I didn't have a curfew, and I could stay out until sunrise. I used to go to the big warehouse raves when perhaps I should have been studying for my school exams. My bestie Amy and I would megadose on Vitamin Bs downed with a massive banana, strawberry, and chocolate shake for energy – this was in the days before energy drinks were a thing. Then we would catch the bus into town and dance all night in one of the warehouses on Wellington wharf. Amy would tell her parents she was crashing at mine so she wouldn't have to meet their curfew. The rave would shut down around 4 or 5 in the morning, and we would walk up the hill, catch the sunrise, and then fall gratefully into our beds until my younger brothers made too much noise for us to sleep in any longer.

During my school days, the dance floor allowed me to escape the responsibilities of being a mother figure to my brothers. On the dance floor, I could shake off all the frustration and confusion that resulted from these responsibilities.

Then, at uni, I found the field raves, and dance allowed me to let my freak flag fly a little. Dancing in the dark with a bunch of bongo-playing hippies felt like my safe space in a world where I was finding who I was.

And then, after five years of studying and a whole lifetime of small-town living, I was ready for the 'big smoke' and moved to London.

Here the anonymity itself felt liberating and gave its own kind of permission. In London, I was on the dance floor most weekends and threw myself into the club scene. Clubbing was where it was cheaper to do drugs than to drink, where I would make new 'best friends' in the communal toilets and dance all night before catching the first tube of the morning home to bed – mine, or my new bestie's.

When I moved to Australia, my primary dance outlet was with the kids in our living room on a Sunday afternoon, dancing to Pete's mixing some of the old anthems on vinyl with some of the latest tracks from Ibiza. Dancing reminded me that I was more than 'Mama'.

The dance floor – whether an official club floor or our living room – was for me a space of limbo.

A space of 'in-between'.

Between the dross of daily life – be that the burden of being a mother figure when I was a teen, the assignments and friendship dramas of my uni days, the boredom of temping in London, or the intensity of domesticity when I became an actual mother - this was the space between my current life and the potential of the life I wanted instead.

Dance allowed me to exist in that in-between space, where I could be me. Just me. That in-between space where I could let go of who I was and start to reach towards who I wanted to be. That in-between space of potential.

But it wasn't until I was no longer at the beck and call of a breastfed baby and started attending a regular Five Rhythms class that I realised what that limbo 'in-between' space was really about. More than potential – it was about permission.

Permission to Just Be

Five Rhythms is a moving meditation of sorts. It is a facilitated free dancing experience founded in 1973 by Gabrielle Roth. It isn't all tie dye and beards, although both are welcome.

It was at Five Rhythms that I realised how powerful permission can be. And also how effing liberating that feels.

On the dance floor, we are given permission to move our bodies in ways that would look weird if there were no music. The darkness on the dance floor gives us permission to not worry about being seen. When we don't worry about being seen, we are given permission to let go, to transform and to shake off any 'big feels'. And, as we discussed in the last chapter, from a physiological perspective, dancing allows us to complete the fear/stress cycle and to move through and release adrenaline.

The part that feels most liberating about Five Rhythms is the space of permission that Honor, my teacher, holds. Sometimes she may directly vocalise it and remind us during the class, and that mere reminder releases a layer of inhibition and reminds me to let go. It reminds me that I am having my own experience. It reminds me that there is no parent standing over my shoulder watching my every move. It reminds me that I am the queen of my own effing destiny.

Other times she doesn't vocalise it, but she just holds such a strong container of permission. And man, does it feel liberating; it's like every cell in my body tingles and is released from that daily holding on, holding in, measuring up.

Lastly, in witnessing everyone else being free with their expression, it allows me to feel free with mine, too. Five Rhythms and dance itself is like a multi-layered cake of permission.

And I'm totally having this cake and eating it, too.

Permission is about acceptance. We all have a basic human need to be seen and heard – not only to be seen and heard but also to be accepted. Accepted in all our colours – in our non-sexy but effing comfortable Bonds underwear, our needing a haircut hair, and our imperfect communication skills. Accepted warts and all.

Really, permission is touching that deep, deep level inside us all, the one that asks 'Am I okay?'

Permission encompasses the complete acceptance of who we are – in all our imperfect shades.

It is permission to be our damn selves.

But Why the Fuck Is Permission Something We Seek Rather Than Just Have?

Let's return to what we learn when we are little humans, specifically what we learn from the big humans around us.

Evolutionary survival depended upon safety in numbers. The more we stayed with our group, our tribe, our community, the safer we remained.

And it was the job of the big humans to ensure that the little humans knew this, knew they needed to stay with the group.

If they wandered, or perhaps even worse, if they were shunned from the group for being too different, well, their chances of survival weren't all that high. Oh, baby, it's a wild world.

Human babies are born perhaps the most helpless of all mammals. Most land-based mammals are usually walking within hours of birth. But humans, bless them, take an average of 12 months to walk independently of their parents. These 12 months are an intense time of neediness and dependency. And it doesn't stop there.

It's in our biology to stay close to our parents and to take our cues from them throughout our childhood. Our biology wants us to survive.

It is the job of the big humans to create and hold safe spaces for us to explore the world. We look to them and our other primary caregivers for their nod of approval, for the 'go-ahead'. We trust that they know this world and that they will keep us safe.

As we grow, we learn what is and isn't considered safe by our parents, and we start to look to them less for the safety check and more for their nod of approval as, still following their lead, we take our own steps into the world.

As we grow from babies into little humans, not only do we hear what our parents say but we also pick up on non-verbal cues, too. And we start modelling ourselves on our parents' values and beliefs.

Remember, it's when we're children that the brain is extra receptive to learning. The things we learn in childhood wire very strongly in our brains.

However, as we grow up, we internalise the voices of our parents. While on the outside we're in big human bodies, on the inside there's still a part of us seeking permission. A little human inside.

The rules of evolution are so etched into our biology that it's like we're literally wired to seek approval and permission before we do something, especially if that something is the kind of thing that might be new to our family.

When we become a big person, this gets interesting and often problematic. We can find ourselves drawn to something that is at odds with, or in contrast to, the way our parents did things and the way we were conditioned to experience ourselves in the world.

It can feel jarring and disconcerting.

Often the things we desire are things that aren't a part of our family story. So, we subconsciously have a need for them to be approved before we can attain them.

The mere fact that something is at odds acts as a block, an obstacle in the way of it becoming a part of our life now. We may desire to leave the 9–5, but if stepping out of the mainstream was not allowed when we were growing up, then we face a conflict.

And when we feel like we aren't allowed to do something, we feel restricted. We want to do it. But we hold back. And that can feel powerless.

When we're liberated from the restrictions, our power increases exponentially.

Yep, exponentially.

I stared nervously at the others on the computer screen, trying to focus on what the coach was saying.

What the fuck was I doing? I had no right to be here.

'Some of you here won't finish your books.' She addressed myself and the five others attending the online meeting.

Oh no, I don't want to be one of those people…but fuck, can I do this?

'It's not about talent, or experience, it's about just writing, every day writing a little bit.'

Oh, but what if it's crap writing and at the end it's just that – a big pile of crap?

'Don't focus on perfection.'

Hmmm, is she reading my mind?

'All you need to do here is a draft. Think of it as a shitty first draft if that helps. That's all I'm asking.'

Woah! Okay, that sounds much easier – doing a shitty first draft rather than a 'book'. I can totally do a shitty first draft.

The nerves started to fade, and in their place arose a tingle of excitement.

I can do this! Phew, this feels like less pressure.

'You guys can do this, but you need to get out of your way and just write.'

Yes!

The tingles of excitement grew at the thought of my own book in my hands.

★

The words 'shitty first draft' were a game changer for me. They gave me permission to just write, to let the thoughts flow without censoring.

I don't know why I needed that permission from someone, but it was the stone that allowed the dam to break and the water to flow freely.

It liberated me from my 'not good enough' thoughts. The permission that Cat, my book coach, gave me allowed me to drop any high expectations of perfection and to let go and let flow.

Why Does Permission Stay Externalised When We Grow Up?

While the world we live in today seems rather permissive, it is in fact quite the opposite in many ways.

Rules and social norms exist to keep us 'in line'. It is within the best interests of society as a whole that we all remain submissive and behave.

Keeping us all domesticated and yielding makes for a much smoother world. Those of us who are parents will know just how much easier things are when our children are behaving. Things are so much quieter, aren't they?

When we're young, our parents are the authority figures. We know what they'll approve of and what they won't. We know what the rules and boundaries are. These of course will vary from family to family, but generally we know what goes, and what doesn't, within our family.

We know that if we do X, then the consequence is Y.

As we grow up, we not only internalise the voices of our parents but also take on the collective voice of society. We internalise what is and isn't acceptable.

Over time, the voices become so ingrained, we don't even realise we have them.

These internalised voices start to sound like 'I can't,' 'I shouldn't,' and 'I'm not allowed to.'

And our brain, our darling, sweet, 'I'm just doing as you tell me' brain listens. She hears these 'can'ts and shouldn'ts and not allowed,' and genie-like, she nods and says, 'Your wish is my command.'

Throw some emotions into the mix and you'll have a heady cocktail of 'fuck this shit o'clock'.

And given that we have historically sought permission from outside of ourselves, it follows that that's why we still have this need now, even though we're 'grownups.'

There's something very powerful about someone giving you permission, whether explicitly like my dance teacher Honor or implicitly like some people in our lives can do without realising.

I dressed carefully, casual jeans with a black top, black boots, black hat, and then lined my lips with a bright red. I wanted to create a good impression.

I arrived early, got myself a drink, and then sat where I could see the door.

I waited. Excited. A bit nervous.

We had been chatting online for a while and had a mutual friend whose party we'd met at years ago, but for some reason we hadn't clicked then. We had become friendly after doing an online class together. Some of the exercises in the class asked us to go deep, to get vulnerable.

Vulnerability was something I always struggled with. This usually carried through to my friendships, where I held back from emotional intimacy or shone the light on the other person rather than sit in it myself. I was a great listener; I was always the one asking probing questions, but I shied away from answering them, often deflecting or distracting with a question that even the least narcissistic couldn't resist.

With Karen, it felt different. I couldn't place my finger on it. Her vulnerability had an edge of fierceness to it; she owned it. She was both vulnerable and strong as fuck. This both scared and thrilled me. But, more importantly, it showed me the possibility.

Perhaps if I were lying on a sofa, Freud might ask me about the connection between vulnerability and weakness and the fact that I grew up with an ill mother. But sorry, Freud, not your book mate.

I saw her before she saw me; she'd dressed carefully, too, and I smiled when I saw she also had bright red lips.

She saw me and grinned and waved.

I got up and gave her an air kiss – because lipstick – and a hug.

'Finally, we get to hang owt!' Gawd her Canadian accent was so cute.

'I know!' I smiled goofily at her.

We talked and drank and ate too many tacos. And I started to fall a little bit in love with her. It felt like a first date. We small talked some history and then went deep into the heart stuff.

And she wanted to hear what I had to say. She dodged my deflections like a pro. And slowly I started to open up.

She was funny, deep, fun, and fierce. She was everything I could want in a new BFF.

But there was something more.

When I got home, I was too buzzed to sleep. I started reflecting on the night and the feelings she gave me.

What was it?

Permission.

She gave me a sense of permission.

She owned who she was – she owned her shadows and her big feels. And she gave me permission to own mine, too.

She gave me permission to be all my shades and contradictions.

And this felt like a new discovery.

Permission Cracks Us Open to Possibility

Permission is the ultimate liberator.

It removes the barriers, the blocks, the things that keep us safe and small.

Permission lifts the sense of powerlessness right off and gives us strength from the inside.

It's a circuit breaker. And when our brain hears it, it realises 'Oh, wow, okay, so we CAN do this? Wow, okay, let's do this, then!' It liberates us from those SLBs and it quiets the fears.

Permission says to that little human inside, 'It's okay, you've got this, you can do this, fly free, it's safe, I got you.'

Do you recall what happened when you did something you weren't allowed to do when you were little?

I should perhaps preface this by saying that I had a privileged as fuck childhood. I grew up in white middle-class New Zealand; sure, there wasn't much money for everything, but we certainly never went without food.

In our family, if we misbehaved, we were disciplined with a smack. One strong whack, through our clothes, on the bottom, by our father.

I can still recall the deep shame I felt when this happened. It wasn't about the pain – it was a firm flat hand over my clothes – it was about the shame.

All these years later, when I think about being smacked, sweaty nausea washes over me. I vowed then that I could never smack my children, not because it was violent, but because I didn't want them to feel that deep sense of shame.

So for me, the consequence of doing something that I was not allowed to do was deep shame.

Brené Brown makes an important distinction between shame and guilt. Guilt is 'I feel bad because I have done a bad thing,' while shame is 'I am a bad person because of the bad thing I did.'

How this manifests now is that when I want something, if I have any inkling that this is something I am not 'allowed' to want, then I start to feel shame. Or I don't even allow myself to want it, because the consequence of doing something I am not allowed to do is shame.

For example, say I wanted a resort-style pool in my garden. But there were some unwritten rules in our family about the kind of people who own pools.

If I broke these rules, I might feel shame.

Heck, I might feel shame just for thinking about breaking those rules.

What I need here is permission.

Being told we *can*, rather than we *can't*, feels both exciting and liberating.

Being told and – actually more powerfully – telling ourselves that we are allowed to do something has a massive impact on our life. Permission makes us stand a little straighter, walk a little taller, lift our little chins higher, and adds a sparkle to our eyes.

'I Am Allowed...'

We have become conditioned to externalising our sources of permission. It's so conditioned that we don't even realise we're doing it. But what if we took the power back and gave *ourselves* permission?

You can be, do, or have *anything* you want!

What if, instead of looking outward, we looked within? And we gave ourselves permission?

After all, if you don't look within, you'll go without.

Your Turn

Go back to your list of desires. Take one and add these four magic words to the front of it:

I am allowed to...

I am allowed to be socially confident in any situation

I am allowed to have a beautiful resort-style pool.

I am allowed to go and live in Italy for three months by myself.

See how that changes things?

Feel that tingle of excitement in your belly and notice how your breath quickens with possibility.

Sometimes permission brings with it the element of surprise. We may be surprised that in giving ourselves permission, we realise that we had in fact been holding ourselves back:

'I can...oh, wait a minute...was I *really* thinking that I couldn't? Gosh darn, well, that's a bit silly, isn't it!'

Play With It

When we engage with permission in this way, it makes us pause, reflect, and notice the stories we have been telling ourselves.

Try adding in a 'not':

I am not allowed to... Because...

See what limiting beliefs come up.

What beliefs serve you?

What things did your parents say about you when you were growing up? How would they describe you as a child? Is this true? Do these descriptions serve you?

I am not allowed to have a resort-style pool because it's a waste of money...because only rich people have them...because people will think I am a snob...because it will be a hassle to clean...

Get Curious

Ask some questions to shift out of the feelings and into the thoughts.

How can I allow myself to receive this?

What would it feel like to allow myself this?

What Comes Up?

See what sneaky limiting beliefs or blocks to receiving are hiding in there.

Are there any themes?

Can you find the origin story – the first time this limiting belief showed up?

Imagine

Find a spot where you won't be disturbed and make yourself comfortable. Close your eyes and allow your breath to gently deepen and slow down.

When you feel relaxed, imagine yourself in some clouds, I'm talking fluffy, bouncy, Care Bear clouds. Notice how supported you feel and what a perfect temperature it is. Notice how relaxed and calm you feel.

As you look around, noting how the light makes the clouds sparkle, you see a shimmer in front of you. Slowly the shimmer takes form, and you see it is a very familiar-looking angel. She smiles at you and says hello, then sits on a cloud in front of you.

She feels like a combination of a caring, fairy tale grandmother and badass goddess.

She tells you she has something for you. She wants you to know that you have permission to be, do, and have whatever the fuck you want.

As she says this, you feel a lightness in your being. Something has been liberated within.

Then she holds out her hand, and in it is a symbol of this feeling for you to keep. A symbol to remind you that you can do whatever the fuck you want.

Smile. Feel this to be true. Thank her and take the symbol.

Shortly she starts to fade into a shimmer again. When you are ready, take some time to bring your awareness again to your breath and your body and, in your own time, open your eyes.

Hack It Daily

- Remind yourself that you are the grownup and you make the rules now. Get something symbolic of this. I have a desk plaque that says 'I'm the MF Boss.'
- Write a Post-it note reminding yourself of this: 'Hey, Natalie, you ARE allowed to be visible on social media!'
- Write a letter to yourself giving yourself permission to do that thing, to try, to fail, to succeed.
    - Letter writing is an awesome practice. I use it weekly as part of my morning writing ritual. Things I have written letters to:
        - Six-year-old me
        - My future clients
        - My social media accounts
        - My fear of speaking up
        - The pain in my back
        - Money
        - Debt
        - Our house

- You can also write a reply, from whoever you wrote the letter to. In creating a dialogue, you are building a relationship with this thing. This in itself is super powerful.
- Seek out people who give you a sense of permission. If you don't know any in real life, then find some on social media to follow.

Too Long; Didn't Read

- We are primed to seek permission from our elders so we remain safe and survive.
- As we grow up, we continue to seek permission from sources outside of ourselves.
- Permission is the ultimate liberator.
- If we give ourselves permission, then we are opening ourselves up to possibility.
- Put 'I am allowed to...' in front of your desires to create a powerful affirmation.

7
'I AM WORTHY...'

I'm holding on to the grass, on all fours, but feeling like I'll fall off the earth if I don't hold on.

Somewhere inside, I know on a rational level that I won't fall off. But still I hold on, fearing what might happen if I do let go.

Shite, here come the tears...

The sobs rise and crash like a big swell. But I can't surf. Hell, I don't even have a surfboard. I just have to flow and ride that wave as best as I can.

It's a deep, deep grief.

You can't do this.

You're not doing this properly.

Who do you think you are, anyway?

Gawd, why am I being so hard on myself?

You're always hard on yourself.

No.

Yep, you're so hard on yourself. You need to stop this.

Why?

Why have I been so awful to myself?

Oh, shit. Here comes another purge.

I turn to the side and retch. My stomach turns inside out again, but all that comes out is a slimy green bile, like snot. My abs are sore from all the retching.

I catch my breath. Close my eyes in relief...and then mermaids. Mediterranean blue, like electric fairies, they swim behind my closed eyes. Looking at me. Beckoning. Their own eyes twinkling.

Open your eyes.

I open my eyes. The grass is so close to my face. Each blade seems to shimmer.

Look at that ant, moving with such purpose.

I am part of this ecosystem, too. We're all so connected. Why do we think we're not?

Wow.

Oh no, here it comes again. A huge wave of a sob crashes over me. I totally understand why it's called a 'wave' of emotion. It crashes over me and I hang on to the grass again.

You have been so cruel to yourself.

You aren't good enough.

Why are you being so cruel to yourself?

I sense someone next to me.

'How are you doing, Natalie? Would you like the Shaman to come and help you?'

Yes.

I can't speak.

I nod. The tears roll down my cheeks.

I am so shit.

Why am I so shit?

Oh, why am I so unkind to myself?

Why am I calling myself shit?

Gawd, I can't even be nice to myself – that's how shit I am.

Why don't I feel good enough?

I am shit.

This is shit.

There's no way I'm doing this again tomorrow. I'll leave as soon as I'm able. I can't believe I put myself through this. It feels like all my moments of trauma in one blow.

It's okay. You can leave in the morning. You don't have to do another day of this.

Oh gawd, more retching.

Snot-green bile again.

I reach for my water, remembering the Shaman saying to drink plenty of water, because the cactus absorbs water.

I swallow the cool liquid in small sips, not wanting to retch again.

A moment of clarity. I look up. Someone is doing yoga five metres away on the hill above; below me someone sits calmly in lotus, her hands open and her face in peace.

Why aren't they hanging onto the earth for dear life?

Like me.

What is wrong with me?

Waves crash; tears drop to the grass.

Then mermaids again, twinkling. Swaying.

And more retching.

Why am I the only one having such a tough time on this? Everyone else can handle it. Fuck, I'm so weak and pathetic. Can't even handle a little psychedelic.

Silver tears.

Blue mermaids.

Snot-green fluid.

Silver. Blue. Green.

Silver.

Blue.

Green.

Silverbluegreen

Eventually she comes, the Shaman. It could have been hours later, or maybe just minutes. She crouches down beside me and asks what's going on.

Mermaids, is all I can answer. And a part of me wants to laugh at myself.

'I can't...' More tears.

'I feel so shit,' I whisper. 'I haven't been very nice to myself.' And then there are more tears.

She asks me if I would like some healing, and when I nod, she tells me to lie on my back.

Slowly I let go of the grass and turn my tender, tender body over, keeping my eyes closed.

Vortex beckons.

Open them; it feels better.

I open them and fark, there's a silver-blue light coming off the Shaman. I cry, but this time without the intense grief.

She pats my whole body with her condor feathers, and the silver light gently fades, taking my pain with it.

I breathe deeper and slower. The waves subside.

I am okay. Everything is okay

A gentle peace covers me like a soft fog and I sit up. The Shaman is gone, and in her place is one of the helpers, holding a bowl of fruit out to me. I smile and take it.

And I sit on the grass in my peaceful fog and slowly and mindfully eat.

I let the sweet juice of the watermelon fill my consciousness and push out the feelings of moments ago. I feel tender, fragile...but the pain has receded.

And it's the best goddamn fruit I've ever had.

In the days leading up to this 'trip' in the Byron Hinterland, I imagined having quite a different experience. I saw myself dancing nymph-like under the sun, barefoot in the grass, moving to some internal melody, with a serene smile on my blissed-out face. I certainly wasn't expecting my first plant medicine experience with Wachuma to be so effing emotional and – if I'm being honest – on the verge of traumatic.

I was worried about the taste and purging, but in the hour between arriving at the house and the ceremony starting, someone told me it was just like a strong green tea.

And it was. In taste.

But in essence, it was like an acid trip while at your therapist's office, fitting ten years of therapy into one session.

It was fucking intense!

Pete had been on one a month earlier. He came back a changed man. His heart was cracked open and he couldn't talk without crying for the first few days. But his tears were happy, heart-expanding ones, not the deep grief-cry of mine.

Even though Pete had had quite the experience on it himself a month earlier, I was sure I would be fine. I mean, I had dealt with so much of my shit. Of course I was going to be fine.

I packed paints and my journal, and my favourite dancing clothes. Nymph barefoot and smiling, remember?

But Wachuma had some other ideas.

Before that 'trip,' I thought I'd dealt with my inner critic. I mean, I knew I had worthiness stuff to deal with. But I thought I was all over the inner critic stuff. I thought she had long gone.

It wasn't until that journey in the Byron Hinterland that I realised... I hadn't in fact dealt with all the layers. Onion-like life is funny like that.

Wachuma highlighted for me that I hadn't sorted out that ole chestnut of mine – self-fucking worth.

Why Do So Many of Us Struggle With This Ole Chestnut?

We are all born worthy.

It's the growing up which fucks us up.

We may be born worthy, but it's conditioned out of us. We receive this conditioning from multiple sources: our parents, our peers, our culture, our governments, and most forms of media. All of this combines to create a collective consciousness.

This collective consciousness tells us we are not enough.

Mainstream media, with its job of marketing to us, needs to first convince us that we are broken. *Then* we are marketable. *Then* we have pain points. *Then* we can be 'fixed'.

Our brain – in doing its 'thang' and gathering info about the world – is very receptive to the messages mainstream media tells us.

'Maybe if you buy this, and buy that, then you'll measure up. Then you'll be enough.'

Translates to:

'Maybe if I buy this and wear that, maybe then I'll measure up. Maybe then I'll be enough?'

But it's not only media which informs collective culture and affects our worthiness. It also comes back to our biology.

Survival of the Fittest

The strongest, the healthiest, the most fertile, the most liked, the ones with the most resources. These are the ones most likely to survive. Everyone else? They don't have enough. This is the feeling that we internalise. This is what drives us; these feelings of lack and 'less than' drive our actions to be, do, and have enough. Because, according to our biology, until we are, do, and have enough, we may not in fact survive.

Much like the stress response of Chapter 5, be it a sabre tooth tiger or a boss's relentless deadline, the brain responds to both situations the same way. The fears of the past, of not measuring up to others in our tribe, trigger the same response as 'not measuring up' does today. Our brain experiences the same feelings as it did when your neighbour was a better hunter than you, as it does when your neighbour has more social media likes than you.

'Crap, they've got more berries than me. Maybe I haven't got enough? Will I survive with what I have?'

'Crap, my Facebook posts don't have as many likes as theirs. I guess people like them more than me; they must be better than me.'

In our quest for survival and to be the fittest, we need to constantly assess ourselves against others.

What was:

Do they have more berries/better shelter/bigger muscles than me?

Is today:

Do they have more likes on social media than me/a better house than me/bigger muscles than me?

Where this assessment becomes problematic is how we interpret it. Does this interpretation leave us feeling better or worse about ourselves?

What Are You Making It Mean?

My phone whistles and tells me I have a text. I pick it up, hoping it's Pete; he's on a different time zone and I miss him.

Him:

Hey Baby! (heart emoji)

Oh yay!

I quickly start typing to catch him before he moves away from wifi and is unreachable again.

Me:

Hey Baby! How are you? Only a few days now, are you excited about coming home?

Him:

I feel ok I guess (downcast eyes emoji)

Um, WTF? I'm excited to see him! Why isn't he excited? Has something happened?

Me:

Oh...?

Him:

Leaving a place with no time and space is hard.

Me:

What don't you like about time and space here at home?

Him:

Plenty (straight lipped blank face emoji)

Ah, fuck. Should I worry? It sounds like he doesn't want to come back home? Shit. This is not cool. Is he going to stay? How will we cope without him? This will break the girls' hearts. My heart feels like it's breaking already. Plus, I've spent a fortune on the snake man since he's been away, three times he's had to come to remove pythons from our chook house... Okay, calm down, Natalie...

Me:

Like...

Please don't say anything about how you've been thinking about your life and the changes you want to make...

Him:

Oh you know. Work responsibilities. The school run. Domestic stuff.

Phew. Okay, it's just life stuff. That's all normal after a month in the mountains of Peru.

Me:

I hear you Baby.

Him:

I am really looking forward to seeing the girls (princess emojis) and you! (eggplant emoji)

We'll stop there as it gets X-rated after that. But my point is this: can you see in the middle there where my shark-week tinged thoughts started running away with my interpretation of his texts?

'What are you making it mean?' is one of my favourite tools for inner enquiry. How I see something might be very different from how someone else sees it. *Everything* about the world is an interpretation, one made through the eyes of the person seeing it.

Everything.

If I had a twin and we spent the day together doing the exact same thing and having the exact same experiences, we would still have different recollections of the day. We would both notice different things, be aware of different things, and analyse things completely differently. She might take the barista's monosyllabic replies personally; I might wonder what had happened in his morning to make him so distant. She might not notice the woman passing by look at us strangely; I might feel the stare and wonder what food I had on my face. She might look at her Instagram page and be happy at the number of followers she had gained that week; I might look at my Instagram and be annoyed at the number of followers I had gained that week.

And the reality? The barista might have lost his voice that day, the woman passing might have stomach cramps, and the number of followers gained might be the exact same number.

Not only do we all see things differently, but our interpretations also fuel our beliefs about ourselves. That is, they support the stories we tell ourselves about ourselves and the world.

What stories are you giving your power to?

Are your worthiness stories supporting beliefs about your limited past? Or are they fuelling beliefs about your future potential?

Feeling Unworthy Is a Huge Block to Receiving

'I want to fly you to the Andamans to meet me for ten days of diving.'

Whoa. I'm in shock. This kind of thing happens in movies, not my life. I don't know what to say.

'Oh wow. Um...'

'Look, I know this is out of the blue,' Pete continues, 'but I've just been double paid, and I'm going to be away for a long time, and this could be a fun way to get to know each other more.'

Shit. I can't accept that. It's too much. I haven't even had sex with this guy yet. I mean, we have done everything else...

'Wow,' I manage, 'I don't know what to say. Um... I really don't know if I can accept that. I mean, it's so kind of you...but...'

'I know it's a bit full on, but just think about it, will you? Sleep on it and let's talk tomorrow.'

In shock, I immediately call my brother.

'Pete wants to fly me to the Andamans!'

'Oh wow, that's awesome!'

'I can't accept that though! I mean, I barely know him, and that's so much money!'

'What?! You're not going to accept a holiday in the Andamans?'

'Yeah, I'm just not comfortable with having that money spent on me.'

'Hmmmm. You might want to think on that, Natalie...'

And so think I did.

A part of me wished that I was the kind of girl who was flown to exotic islands by generous men. Another part felt shite that I didn't have the money to fly myself right now – I was in the start-up, pre-celebrity days of my massage work and funds were tight.

But the more I enquired within, the more I realised it was because I didn't think I was worth it. Little ole me, a Kiwi in the big smoke that is London, struggling to pay rent on her shoebox studio flat in Bayswater.

And as I sat there thinking about it, something shifted and I started wondering, why not?

Why not little ole me? Why can't I say 'Yes'? What would happen if I did? How would that feel?

The thought took my breath away, in that sharp intake which happens when you are pleasantly surprised. And I started to open up to the possibility. The more I played with the 'what if,' the more the idea grew on me.

A few hours later, I called Pete and accepted.

Our time in the Andamans was magic. He ended up with an ear infection after our first dive, so it was more beach time than dive time. But we went from a date once or twice a week in London to ten days of 24/7 on a tropical island. It was the beginning of the falling in love, that sweet limbo of butterflies and post-sex talk into the early morning.

Five months later, I was expecting the baby we accidently made – you'll hear more of that story in Chapter 9.

And 11 years later, we are living in our dream home in Australia with two daughters, seven alpacas, and eight chickens.

What would have happened if I hadn't accepted that offer to be flown to the Andamans? If I had listened to the feeling of not being 'worthy'? Where would I be today?

'I Am Worthy'

On the path to our desires, let's start telling ourselves that we *are* worthy of them. Let's counteract the shitty messages of mainstream media and our damn biology telling us otherwise.

Let's step up into our worthiness.

Because, my beauty, you *are* worthy. You are as worthy as Beyoncé and Lady Gaga and Oprah. You are worthy of all the things on your list of desires. Every single one of them.

Every. Single. One.

Think of the times in your life when you pushed through a belief and something awesome happened. Really think for a moment about those moments when you stood on that threshold or at a fork in the path. If you hadn't pushed through, what might your life look like now?

Now, let's turn this around: what things could you push through today? What possibilities could be awaiting beyond today?

Imagine if you felt worthy enough to be/do/have that thing on your desire list that feels like an impossibility. Who would that person be?

Your Turn

Add these four words to the front of your heart's desires:

I am worthy of...

I am worthy of having a resort-style pool.

I am worthy of being confident in all social situations.

I am worthy of making more than enough money.

How does that feel?

What comes up?

Play With It

Add a 'not' in there and see what comes up. See what sneaky limiting beliefs are hiding in there about your apparent worthiness or unworthiness.

I am not worthy of having a resort-style pool because...

Can you get to the origin?

Keep going until you hit the sweet spot, the a-ha moment, the 'manicured nails wtf' realisation.

Get Curious

Ask some questions to shift out of the feelings and into the thoughts.

What would someone who feels worthy of these desires do tomorrow when they woke up?

How would someone who felt worthy of these desires walk?

How would someone who felt worthy of these desires talk about themselves and their life?

What little actions could you take towards becoming that person today?

What Comes up?

How does it feel to put yourself in the shoes of someone who feels completely worthy of their desires?

Are there any themes or sneaky limiting beliefs revealing themselves?

Imagine

Close your eyes. Become aware of your breath. Allow some spaciousness into your breath. Allow your inbreath to expand. And allow your outbreath to soften.

Feel your body drop and let go.

Allow yourself to release and relax.

You are completely safe.

Imagine yourself walking in a forest, a gentle morning light-dappled forest. There is bird song, the gentle hush of trees swaying in a slight breeze.

The temperature is perfect.

And you walk at a pace which is comfortable for you.

You can hear the melody of a small river. You follow the path and around a corner see the sun sparkling on the water. There are three big, flat stepping stones, and you easily cross the small river.

On the other side, there is a small incline, and the path winds up a gentle rise.

As you walk, the forest clears and you turn the last corner and come to a small grassy area. In the middle there is a big white rock, and on the rock something shines and twinkles as the sun catches it.

As you get closer, you see that it is a crown.

You stand in front of it, and you know that it is yours.

Gently take it and place it on your head. Feel its soft, reassuring weight, and know that you are worthy of this crown.

Hack It Daily

Find a photo of yourself as a baby, when you haven't yet been spoiled by the collective culture. Let it remind you that you are worthy, just as you are.

Place an invisible crown on at times when you feel your worth is going to be tested, like when you are at a social gathering or scrolling Instagram.

Curate your social media!

- This is a big one. Social media is the latest invention and expression of the collective culture. So be aware of what messages you are opening yourself to receiving as you scroll. Is your feed full of fitness mamas? Do they inspire you or make you feel crap?

- Have a scroll and see how you feel as you look. Try to step back and listen to the voices in your head as you do so. I just tried this and man, it's hard. Thoughts I noticed were: 'Oh wow, she is launching another business...damn, I didn't look that good when I was pregnant.. I wish my kitchen looked like that... Oh, that's beautiful art...' Only the last observation made me feel good.

- It's the feelings behind the observations that are important. Do you feel good or bad?

- You can also create a virtual vision board on your social media using the 'Save posts' functions. Save things that fall into your 'be, do, and haves.'

- Finally, please remember to use your social media mindfully. Be conscious of your consumption of social media. Remember that world experts are working on ways to keep you consuming and the platforms and apps are designed to be addictive. They use psychology of gambling to find ways of keeping you there longer than you intend, so be gentle with yourself and do what you need to do to reduce your consumption.

You can also curate the ads shown to you while you are on social media.

- Do a search in Facebook for things you love, and then see what things Facebook shows you. I did this recently for electric cars and holidays to the Maldives, so instead of a course on funnels, Facebook was showing me ads for electric cars and the Maldives. It made for a much nicer scrolling experience.

Too Long; Didn't Read

- We are all born worthy.
- The collective culture thrives on us feeling unworthy.
- Our worthiness comes into question when, driven by the biological drive of 'survival of the fittest,' we compare ourselves to others around us.
- How we interpret our comparisons is important.
- Our interpretations fuel our beliefs about ourselves and support the stories we tell about ourselves.
- Feeling unworthy is a block to receiving.
- Add 'I am worthy' in front of your desires to create a kickass affirmation.
- What would you walk/talk/act like if you felt worthy of your biggest desires?

8
'I AM GRATEFUL...'

I duck down to go through the small doorway into the mud hut.

It always takes a few moments for my eyes to adjust to the darkness. Once I can see, I find my usual spot and sit on the dry, dusty floor.

Sandra follows me and sits in her spot. The family is already seated and waiting for us.

Amma starts serving up the food. She serves her husband first and he eagerly starts to eat. She then serves Sandra and I, as we are the guests. Taking my plate, I nod and smile my thanks. After serving her children and mother-in-law, Amma finally serves herself. I always wait until she has her own before I start eating.

I stare down at the rice and dahl on my plate. I don't feel very hungry, but I slowly start gathering the rice into a ball with my fingers and scooping up some dahl with it. I am used to eating with my fingers now; it feels quite natural.

This has been my breakfast and dinner every day for two months straight. Very occasionally I walk the half hour to the Lake, where there are some tourist restaurants, and savour some other flavours.

But most days it is just 'dahl baht' – dahl and rice, twice a day. Day in, day out.

It is cooked fresh daily. This is Amma's job, cooking for her family. Her family consists of her husband, three children, and her mother-in-law. And for the last two months she has also had Sandra and I to cook for, two teacher trainers in training.

I had been in Nepal for three months. The first month I trekked the Annapurna Circuit in the Himalayas. These last two I had been with this family, learning teacher training, working on my Nepali, and eating the same thing every damn day.

After two months of it for breakfast and dinner, I'm craving something else. The thought of more dahl makes me feel sick. I want to push it aside and curl up in a ball in my sleeping bag and not see anyone all day.

As an introvert by nature, being constantly around people is hard. When we walk through the villages to schools, everyone stares. In this country, we are the 'exotic other'. Our fair skin and my bottle blonde hair are novelties. I feel observed, on show, and this makes it hard for me to relax.

Even now I can feel the family looking at me, wondering why I'm eating so slowly.

I keep balling the rice and dahl with my fingers and slowly bringing it to my mouth. After only a few mouthfuls, I feel done.

How can they eat the same meal twice a day every fucking day?

I want to stop eating, but I can't leave food on my plate. That would feel ungrateful.

Sandra catches my eye and raises a concerned eyebrow in question.

I give her a small, tight smile and nod.

It's okay. I've got this.

When I start feeling this way, I know it's a sign that I need some space.

Perhaps after breakfast I'll walk into town and hire a long boat. I could sit on the end and row right into the middle of the lake. The people would become tiny dots on the shore and it would be still and quiet. No one looking at me, no one talking to me. I could lie in the boat and count my blessings.

Jeez, Natalie. Count your fucking blessings now. Look at where you are.

A confusing mixture of shame, pain, and frustration washes over me.

Shame, because I 'shouldn't' be feeling this – coming from such a privileged background.

Pain at the conflict between these feelings and my 'shoulds'.

And frustration over the conflict and the subsequent harsh judging of myself.

Gotta get out of my head!

I take a deep breath. I'm not going to let my inner judge get the better of me.

My feelings are valid. There is no need to judge them.

My shoulders soften a little and the frustration starts to dissipate.

What can I use as a circuit breaker here?

I scan through my mental toolbox...

Gratitude. That's always a good one.

I am grateful that I have food. I am grateful that the board I pay helps this family. I am grateful that we do the best to communicate even though their English is minimal and my Nepali isn't great. I am grateful that I have the amazing Sandra here with me. I am grateful that I have been given the opportunity of a lifetime. I am grateful that I am privileged enough to be able to be here. I am grateful for the laughs we have with the family. I am grateful that we are entertaining to this family – although sometimes it's hard to tell if they are laughing with us or at us.

My breathing slows and I feel lighter.

Okay, that's better.

I catch Sandra's eye again and smile. She returns it with her own relieved smile.

Now eat your fucking rice, girl!

The last of the food is surprisingly easy to swallow. I finish and then raise my head to smile my thanks at Amma.

She is looking at me with her own questioning look, as I am the last to finish.

'*Yo ramro cha,*' I say, smiling at her and showing her my empty plate, patting my belly with the other hand.

They all laugh. Perhaps they are laughing with me, or perhaps at me. Either way, I laugh along with them.

Gratitude is such a powerful circuit breaker. It's one that never fails me, whether trying to finish my plate in a mud hut in Nepal or feeling annoyed at something Pete has done.

But gratitude wasn't always so accessible to me.

My first experiences of gratitude were not positive associations. They were filled with guilt and confusion. The gratitude of my childhood was about being grateful for what we had relative to those less fortunate than us.

I recall many a childhood meal when I pushed the over-cooked broccoli around my plate and tried to hide it under a pile of mash.

'Est-ce que je peu quitte la table s'il vous plaît?' I carefully pronounced the words, hoping it would distract my parents from the food remaining on my plate.

My mother smiled. The French was her doing. I think she was living out her alter ego via us; she was fluent and we had the odd smattering of phrases.

But my father, unimpressed by my words, tutted his disapproval.

'No, Natalie, you may not leave the table!' he said. 'There are children in Africa who would be so grateful to have half of what you have left on your plate. Eat it up, please.'

I didn't understand. What did my appetite have to do with those children in Africa? If I didn't want it, couldn't we just send it to them? Because I wasn't hungry. *I'd* had enough.

Perhaps this is a generational thing – I was a child of the '80s, and the Ethiopian famine was the biggest crisis of the first half of that decade. The news was filled with sparrow-limbed children with distended stomachs, so malnourished that they couldn't lift their arms to wave away the flies crawling on their face. This was distressing for me to see, and I imagine my parents, with four of their own children to feed, also felt an uncomfortable cocktail of emotion – guilt stirred with gratitude topped with a splash of shame. Guilt that their children had food when others were starving. Gratitude that it was someone else's children who were suffering. And shame for feeling the latter.

It confused me.

Did grateful mean I should eat beyond feeling full?

In my childhood years, gratitude carried with it an association of guilt and confusion. Was I supposed to ignore my body's cues of 'fullness' and keep eating and then feel grateful? Is that what gratitude was about? Did I need to be overeating because others couldn't eat?

I *was* grateful. I just wasn't hungry.

It wasn't until I reached my teens and the power of gratitude started being bandied about by Oprah and other daytime talk show hosts that it was reframed for me.

I started to connect gratitude to a different feeling: to the feeling of being thankful.

The thankful of my adult years was different from my childhood. It wasn't about guilt and too full bellies, and it didn't feel like the sharp pinch of shame for not only having more food than I needed, but also feeling like I was wasting it.

The thankful of my adult years became a different kind of cocktail of feelings altogether. It was a double shot of joy stirred with mindfulness and topped with a dash of deep peace.

It was a feeling and an energy that I could tap into and use to access a better part of myself.

And I soon realised that this kind of gratitude was one of the quickest ways to change my thoughts and shift my mood.

Gratitude Itself Is Powerful AF

We are actually wired to be grateful and kind. When we experience gratitude or kindness the brain is flooded with dopamine, which results in a natural high. Perhaps this is Mama Nature's way of encouraging us to be kinder and more grateful?

Essentially, in order to survive, we need to stay connected to others. Our physiology ensures this by rewarding us for those connections. When we reach out to others in kindness, our biochemistry rewards us with a rush of chemicals that feel good. We want more of this good feeling, so we do it again.

There is bucket-loads of research today about how amazing gratitude is for us humans.

Psychologists Emmon and McCullough found that keeping a gratitude journal not only enabled people to feel more positive about themselves but also affected their health positively. They asked three groups to keep a daily journal for ten weeks. One group was instructed to note the things for which they were grateful. Another group was instructed to note the things which annoyed them. And the last group was instructed to just write, with no focus on either positive or negative events. Those in the gratitude group reported feeling more positive about their lives and had fewer visits to the doctor, too.

Two studies by a Professor Mills found a big correlation between gratitude and heart health. In the first study, with two gratitude journaling groups, he discovered that higher levels of gratitude were associated with better mood, better sleep, and less inflammation. In his next study, he found that patients keeping gratitude journals showed significant reductions in the biomarkers that indicate increased risk of heart failure. He concluded that a 'grateful heart is a healthier heart.'

In this chapter, we will take a deep dive into the three 'most relevant to this book' ways that gratitude is powerful:

1. Gratitude can quickly change our emotional state.
2. Gratitude keeps us in the present moment, and the present moment is where joy lives.
3. Gratitude opens us up to receiving.

Gratitude Changes Our Emotional State

Gratitude is a wonderful mental circuit breaker, and it can quickly change our emotional state.

It is one of the most effective circuit breakers when you are in a negative-feeling state, such as fear or sadness, or if you have spiralling negative thoughts.

Gratitude shifts the patterning on a neural level and activates other parts of our brains. We shift from the firing and wiring of 'worry' and move into the firing and wiring of 'appreciation.'

In this way, gratitude can quickly shift us from a fear state to a relaxed state. Anxiety, fear, or worry can all trigger a stress response. You will recall from Chapter 5 what happens when we are in fear

– our sympathetic nervous system is activated and we fall into 'flight or fight.'

When we are worried about something, our thought patterns can become dominated by going through worst-case scenarios. Our poor brain is just trying out all the 'what-ifs' – so it can figure out how we would handle each one were it to happen. And remember, the brain cannot tell the difference between what is happening outside our body – in the world around us – and what is happening inside our head – in our overactive and easily stress-triggered imagination.

When we step back and take control of our *thinking* brain, and start to direct the thinking, then we can affect our physiology. When we stop thinking of the worrying things and instead focus on the things we're grateful for, then our parasympathetic nervous system is activated, and we feel relaxed.

Just like I used gratitude as a circuit breaker when I was feeling in a funk in a mud hut in Nepal, it can be a wonderful way to shift your thinking, especially if your thinking is the beginning of a spiral into those unhelpful thoughts and beliefs and their accompanying emotions.

Gratitude Focuses Us in the Present Moment

Gratitude encourages mindfulness. When we consciously put ourselves in a state of appreciation, we are giving our brain a task, asking it to focus on finding things to be thankful for. It takes us out of worries about the future and stress of the past, into the present moment.

The present moment is all there really is. And the more we can sit and rest in that moment, the happier we will be. Being in the moment asks us to slow down, to look with new eyes at the world around us, and to recognise all the goodness in this moment:

Currently it's 10:26 on a Saturday morning. I'm at the end of the kitchen table, my computer surrounded by piles of papers, notes, and books. The house is quiet; Pete's taken the girls hiking. To my left is a wall mostly of windows; outside is a sea of green – palms and trees tower over the house, a few flashes of purple from the lilies on the dam. I can hear birds and a motorbike in the distance. To my right is our kitchen; there's an abundance of fruit in the fruit bowl. The remains of last night's dinner of homemade pizza clutter the counter.

As I look around, I smile. I am so effing lucky, and life is so effing awesome right now. If I move into the future, I might start to wonder about my week, the to-do list, the chiro appointments I need to make for my back that is niggly, the small fears around Pete's career pivot and the uncertainty that wants to arise when I think about that. And if I move into the past, I might start to go over business decisions I made last week that I'm second guessing, things I forgot to do and the stress that arises when I think about that.

Even just writing about the future and the past gives me a twinge of adrenaline and I can feel the accompanying thoughts want to take hold. So, give me a moment while I gaze out the window and return to that place of now, of peace, the swaying palms, the quiet house, and the kitchen table cluttered with my sweet and simple life.

★

Mindfulness is promoted by many health professionals as a way of coping with mental health challenges. I believe that gratitude can do the same, because gratitude brings with it feelings of appreciation, and appreciation sits close to happiness.

In *Ask and It Is Given,* Esther Hicks teaches what she calls a 'rampage of appreciation'. This is a very quick way to shift into a higher vibrational state – into a state that feels better. The idea is to look around randomly throughout the day and find an object that pleases you. Notice and appreciate why it pleases you, then you move to another, and another.

For instance: the bowl on top of the pile of books to my right is a gorgeous Japanese one I bought myself at a GOMA on a recent childfree trip to the city. I love eating out of it, and if I look closely I can see how each marking on it is unique. The colours and the shapes are so delicate; I love whoever created it. My eyes move to my pencil; it's gold and with white writing spelling out 'You are gold baby, solid gold.' I love how shiny it is and wonder who came up with the idea; I thank them for the smiles they give me when I use that pencil and take the time to read and feel its message. This table, a varnished wood bargain that Pete picked up for a crazy $50 – it was 10% its original price as it was floor stock. This table has been ours since our girls were babies; it's held so much nourishment for our family. It's also held space for our dinner time discussions, and now it is holding space for this book. I love this table...

Stop reading and try this right now. Look around you and give each object some love. See how you feel afterwards.

Don't keep reading.

Seriously, stop and do the exercise. It will take less than a minute, but its effects will last hours.

Gratitude Opens Us to Receiving

Gratitude is usually only felt in relation to something that has happened. Notice the past tense – happened.

A good thing happens – we are grateful.

We could say that gratitude carries with it the emotional signature of a sense of 'already-happened-ness.' It carries with it the vibration of something already manifested.

When we sit in the air of something already happened, how does it feel? As opposed to waiting for that thing to happen?

Let's return to our top BDHs:

How does it feel thinking about being/doing/having that thing in the future versus feeling how it feels to *already* be/do/have that thing?

Notice that tingle in your body? That simultaneous letting go of tension and embracing of joy. This is the power of gratitude.

This is broadcasting energetically that it has already happened. This is so simple, but so powerful.

On a brain level, we are switching from the limiting belief-triggering pattern of 'but when and how?!' to the limitless belief-triggering pattern of 'it's here already.'

By being grateful, we open ourselves up to receiving more of a good thing.

Grateful Loving Kindness Practice

The morning sun streams in my kitchen window and lights up the most perfect me-sized spot on the floor. I stand in it and choose my song.

I place my hand on my heart and think of someone I am grateful for in my life.

Today my mother appears. This is a relationship that triggers some unhelpful stories.

Hmmm, too hard to start; let's have another, please.

My daughters appear.

Easy.

I open my eyes and press play.

It takes a moment for the Bluetooth to connect and then the room is filled with upbeat music.

Instantly I smile. I start to move, and I think of my daughters.

I am grateful for their cuddles. I am grateful for their fierceness. I am grateful for what they have brought to my life. I am grateful for their fart jokes and the way they tell me about their day. I am grateful for their giggles and their big smiles.

The music and the gratitude amalgamate within me and I start to feel the joy simmer and then bubble over.

Yes! I feel good now.

And the gratitude turns to a simple love, and I start to send that their way.

May they feel deeply happy. May they feel supported. May they be surrounded by people that love and care for them. May they smile more every day.

Now I can turn to my mother.

The energy of gentle love running through my body buffers me this time.

I am grateful for her role in my existence. I am grateful for her creativity and love of art that she nurtured in us. I am grateful she took us to so much theatre. I am grateful for all the places around the world she took us to. I am grateful for her expression of herself – pink hair and big rings and statement jewellery. I am grateful she didn't subscribe to the mainstream media's beliefs about how women should look.

Deep breath.

And now I send her love and I wish her joy.

May she be happy. May she laugh more every day. May she be in the best health. May she be surrounded by love.

My whole being fills with joy and I smile. Then I move onto the rest of my family, my father – wishing him good health and joy; my brothers: the eldest – love and joy and peace to him; the middle – love and joy and calm to him; and the youngest – love and joy and wonder to him.

I spend the rest of the song in a beautiful loop of my own happiness, sending that happiness to others and in turn making myself feel happier.

The last moments, I turn that inward to myself.

May I be happy. May I be in optimum health. May I be full of peace. May I continue to live in good vibes as my default state.

And I take a few moments to see myself in my current desires. Laughing with our family around the pool. Receiving emails from people who have had their lives changed from my work. Driving my Tesla.

This last bit is my twist. In linking or hooking these good feelings to my desires, I am creating and strengthening the neurological wiring. I want to feel so good about my desires that my brain has that association of 'feel good' attached to thoughts of my desires.

It was only recently I discovered the Buddhist practice of loving kindness meditation and added it with a twist to my own gratitude practice. There is something that feels so good about sending other people love and peace and good wishes.

On a neurological level, *we* have to be in a good emotional state to think of *others* in a positive state. But the mere act of thinking of others alone acts as a circuit breaker in itself. Both a circuit breaker and a trigger.

It can break a neural circuit of unhelpful thinking – i.e. beliefs and stories that don't serve you – that you are addicted to on a neurological level purely because their wiring is so strong that it's like a default way of thinking.

And it can also trigger a new physiological cycle. It triggers the flood of endorphins in the body. Thinking happy thoughts triggers the body to feel happy feelings.

Sadly, it is much, much easier to think happy thoughts about others than it is to think them about ourselves. Thinking about someone else is less complicated and loaded than thinking about yourself can be.

When we try to 'circuit break' some negative thinking to think happier thoughts about ourselves, often other thoughts can get in the way. The 'hows' and the 'shoulds' start to rear their not so pretty heads:

'How the F am I supposed to feel happy when we don't know where next month's rent is coming from?'

'Why me? Why am I the one working so hard for my money when everyone else seems to be earning more than me but working less?'

'How can I be happy when I'm living in a body like this?'

'I can't think happy thoughts; my toxic relationship with my mother/weight that I can't lose/business failures get in the way.'

But when thinking about someone else, we don't have all that stuff or baggage around them. Note: if everyone in your life triggers you, then you can start with thinking about someone you don't know very well – a woman who serves you at your local cafe, someone you follow on Instagram, or even a random stranger.

It's lovely to do this in public. It feels like being an undercover creator of high vibes. I like to do it on the train, or walking in a shopping mall, or lying on the beach. I look at the random people around me and I send them love and wish them happiness. It really can be done anywhere and it's a sure-fire way to get in a high vibe state of mind.

And if the baby chicks from Chapter 3 are anything to go by, then our good thoughts directly affect the people we're thinking about.

Like many things, it's best to do this quickly, to linger only as long as it feels good. As soon as you feel an inkling that other, not so helpful thoughts are arising, then move the fuck on.

'I Am Grateful...'

When we add these words in front of our desires, we make a powerful affirmation that taps into the energy of gratitude. It helps shift your emotional state to one of appreciation as well as confidence. You're telling your brain that your desire has already happened. This cues your brain to relax and to 'feel good' about this desire.

Reaching our desires feels fucking awesome. And if you can tap into that feeling of them already being achieved, you are helping your brain to feel much more comfortable with the idea of something that currently may trigger fear or unhelpful beliefs.

Remember, your brain can't tell the difference between something that is happening inside via our thoughts or outside via our interpretation of the world. So, give your brain that confidence boost and feel good around your desires.

With gratitude, you've jumped to the end point – the feeling past the point in the middle that can feel messy with fears, limiting beliefs and unhelpful stories around our worth. It's like giving your brain hope, exposing it to the possibility and potential of those desires and the feelings you'll have once the desires are realised.

Feelings are effing powerful, and used wisely they can change your life – this is what we will dive into in the next chapter.

For now, take your chosen desires and see how it feels to add these three or four words in front of them.

Your Turn

Put 'I am so grateful for...' in front of your BDHs.

I am so grateful to have an exceptional work–life balance.

I am grateful to be in amazing physical health.

I am so grateful to have my website complete and published.

How does that feel?

For me, it makes me smile.

Your brain is hearing that it has already happened, and the feelings are triggered as if that were true.

Play With It

Adding some qualifiers in front of any BDHs that feel too big is a great way to ease yourself into them.

I am open to the idea of...

I am willing to see the possibility of...

It is possible for me to...

I can see myself feeling grateful about...

One day soon I will be/do/have...

I am open to embracing the thought of...

Qualifiers are a great middle ground as you slowly build up to stepping into receivership of your desires. Remember that affirmations are a way of making the unfamiliar become familiar. The more ways we become comfortable with the things we want to be, do, and have, the more quickly we will actually be, do, and have them. Sometimes, going straight to 'I have a Tesla' can feel too far and unfamiliar; we may need to affirm 'I am open to the idea of having a Tesla' for a while before we are comfortable with the idea itself.

What Comes Up?

When you play with the qualifiers, what comes up for you?

Any sneaky limiting beliefs in the form of doubts?

Remember, everything is happening *for* you, not *to* you.

Get Curious

Ask some questions to shift out of the feelings and into the thoughts.

How would it feel to already have this?

Imagine

Get comfortable sitting or lying somewhere you won't be disturbed.

Close your eyes and bring your awareness to your breath. Don't change it; just allow it to soften and deepen a fraction, just by your mere awareness of it.

Now visualise yourself as you were ten years ago.

Recall what stage of your life you were in and what was going on in your world – both inner and outer world.

Where were you living? What were you doing for money? Who were you hanging out with?

Now think of a few things you were doing back then that you are reaping the benefits from today.

These could be things to do with your health, your finances, your relationships.

Perhaps you put some money aside? Perhaps you completed a degree? Perhaps you travelled? Perhaps you went through a heartbreak but survived.

Be creative and see what comes to mind.

Now turn to that ten-year-ago self and give thanks. Thank it for doing these things, things that may have been hard, or boring, or just things you got through.

They don't have to be big things. Life-changing things can be small.

Once you have thanked your past self, take a few deep, slow, gentle breaths and let go of the vision of that self.

Now envision yourself ten years into the future. Imagine a future where your dreams and goals have been realised. Where all your bes, dos, and haves are a part of your daily life.

See the future you that lives this magical life on a daily basis. What do they look like? Is your future self dressed any differently? What do you notice about your future self – both physically and beyond the physical? How are they holding themselves? What do their daily rituals and habits look like?

Now see your future self turn to you and start thanking *you*. They are thanking you for all the little things that you did to help them get to where they are now.

Pay attention to, and make note of, the things you are being thanked for.

These things are keys, clues if you like, from your future self – keys to getting there quickly. Keys to becoming your future self much more quickly.

Once you feel you have received everything you are meant to from your future self, thank them.

Now, slowly bring your awareness back into your body, into the present day, into the right here and right now.

Grab a pen and paper and make a few notes. Jot down the things that your future self thanked you for.

When I did this, mine thanked me for pushing through the fear, for the little daily actions, for not giving up, for tacking comparisonitis, for believing it was possible, even when the current physical evidence said otherwise.

She gave me the encouragement I needed and she showed me what was possible.

Imagining her and building a relationship with her allowed me to tap into feelings of motivation.

It's often only in retrospect that things make sense. This exercise is a way of tapping into the 'sense-making space' earlier.

You can do this as often as you like. Developing a relationship with your future self is a beautiful and valuable practice.

Hack It On the Daily

Act from your future self. How would your future self walk? Drive? What would they do after dinner? How would they write emails?

Project yourself into the future and give gratitude for all that you currently have and all that your past self (your now self) did for you.

Create your version of loving kindness meditation. Put some of your favourite tunes on; turn them up loud and just go for it. Dance, sway, or be still. Imagine and think fondly of people that you know and love, or those that you don't know. Add your gratitude for your desires at the end, as if they are already a part of your current reality.

Recite your daily gratitudes in your head before you fall asleep at night. Big and small, whether a 'contract signed' or 'my daughter's dimple'. Then end with a few gratefuls about your future desires – give thanks as if you already have them. Because you are close to sleep, your brain waves are starting to slow, and as you'll remember from Chapter 1, when your brain waves slow you are more receptive to new thoughts.

You could also have a nightly check-in with your future self: see if she has any advice for you. Maybe she'd like to take over your gratefuls. You might be surprised by what she's grateful for you doing for her today.

Create a vision board and make sure to include some photos both of things you already have that you are grateful for and some pictures of yourself – it's important that your brain sees you next to the things that you desire to be, do, and have.

Once you have created a vision board, save a photo of it as your screensaver on your phone or computer. You can also print it out and keep small copies of it in your car, your wallet, on your fridge, on your bathroom mirror, or above a light switch you use daily. Seeing it in as many places as possible helps your brain to normalise it. Each time you see it, say 'Thank you!' and feel how freaking awesome it's going to be to be, do, and have everything on it.

Too Long; Didn't Read

- Gratitude is an awesome circuit breaker and can change our emotional state.
- Gratitude keeps us in the present moment, and the present moment is where joy lives.
- Gratitude opens us up to receiving because it carries with it the energy of 'already happened'.

9
'I AM SO FUCKING...'

The tiles were cool on my feet as I slowly crept through the villa. The frescoed walls looked even more dreamy at this time of night. I carefully opened the back door so as not to wake anyone else and walked across the soft grass.

Oh wow, this scene feels like a dream.

The full moon was reflected perfectly on the still surface of the pool. When I reached the tiles at the edge, I loosened the belt on my gown, then let it slip from my shoulders and fall to my feet. The midsummer night air was soft against my bare skin. I raised my hands above my head and dove into the water. It was warm and silken against my body. When I came up in the middle of the pool, I flipped to my back, floating, and took it all in.

Wow. What a moment. I can't believe I'm finally here.

This was the moment that I had been waiting for, for the last six intense months of writing my thesis. I had pinned a map up on the wall by my desk in the office adjoining my professor's and I made little flags to pin in the places I wanted to visit.

These little pins kept me going through research and rewrites. When all my friends were enjoying their summer off and celebrating their exams being done and dusted, I sat at my desk and – fuelled by that map – wrote.

I wrote about the way in which the media impacts women's self-esteem and body confidence, and I imagined myself trekking in Nepal. I wrote about studies that found links between current fashion trends and eating disorder patterns, and I imagined myself exploring Italy. I wrote about my own study, which found a link between the size of fashion models women look at and their feelings about their own body and self-esteem, and I imagined myself snowboarding in the French Alps.

The little pins in all the places I wanted to visit kept me sane and helped me to finish the damn thesis.

And now, under a full moon, on the other side of the world, I was in one of those places – Tuscany.

I had done it. I had finished my master's, I had left New Zealand, and this was the beginning of the next phase of my life. I was done with academia; it was now time for adventures.

I smiled to myself and felt a rush of excitement through my body. What a beginning, in an amazing frescoed villa in Italy.

Whoa, what the fuck is that?

Tiny magical dots of light. Flickering around the pool like fairies. They were in the hedges at the edge of the pool, darting around the leaves. I had never seen them in real life, only in Disney movies.

Here I was, skinny dipping under a full moon, in Tuscany, with fucking fireflies.

Fuck yes!

This was a moment.

This was a 'fuck yes' moment.

And there, under the glow of the moon, I promised myself that I would fill my life with such moments, with fuck yes moments.

And so I started to collect them.

Eating the most sublime pasta on a Tuscan terrace, overlooking grape vines as far as the eye can see – *fuck yes.*

Catching the last chairlift of the day, smoking a joint at the top while the slopes emptied and then snowboarding alone down a mountain in the French Alps – *fuck yes.*

Standing in front of a real-life Klimt at the Belvedere in Vienna – *fuck yes.*

Wearing wings and glitter and dancing in a field at Glastonbury – *fuck yes.*

Battling altitude sickness and reaching the Peak of the Annapurna circuit in the Himalayas in a three-week trek – *fuck yes.*

Being flown to Barcelona for dessert – *fuck yes.*

Drinking sweet mint tea in Marrakech by a pool lit by floating candles – *fuck yes.*

I collected these moments like jewels. Jewels that I could bring out when I needed a touchstone. I could pull one from my memory, like reaching into a velvet bag of polished crystals – pick one and roll it in my hand and recall it. Recalling these moments gave me an instant rush of 'fuck yes!' These moments were wired into my brain. When I remembered them, my 'fuck yes' neurons fired.

When I entered the phase of 'sleepless nights spent with a milky breathed tiny human,' aka parenthood, the moments changed. They weren't so worldly, but they were still there:

Feeling my fierce and the energy of the universe coming out of me as I birthed my daughter in a pool in our living room – *fuck yes*.

Doing a dawn fire ceremony on our new build site – *fuck yes*.

Grooving with my bestie at a Tash Sultana concert in the late summer sun – *fuck yes*.

The air thick with sage and incense and my lover topless drumming and clearing the energy in our new house – *fuck yes*.

Sitting in the early morning warm winter sun watching fog clear over our land and eating toast with avocados from our own damn tree – *fuck yes*.

All of these moments are touchstones. They are moments I can return to which instantly give me a rush of that 'fuck yes' feeling.

I hope that by now, nine chapters into this book, you understand the power of your brain and some of the ways you can make the complexities of your brain work in your favour. You know how your beliefs and stories are created and you know that their pull is strong because they are thickly wired in your brain. You realise that some of these beliefs may be so subtle that they are in fact holding you back in life. But you know that it is within your power to change this.

In this final chapter, I am going to talk about the most powerful way you can connect your *thinking* and your *feeling* brain so that you can have the life you desire. To begin with, I'll tell you all about the important role that emotions play in the firing and wiring in your brain. Then I'll explain how you can stay in the 'fuck yes' and avoid the abyss of 'but how?!' Lastly, I'll introduce you to the power of swearing. By the end of this chapter, you'll see swearing in a whole new light.

Let's fucking do this!

Emotions Are Indicators of Significance

Memories, like beliefs, are formed with meaning. The more meaningful something is, the more likely we are to remember it.

Emotion also creates meaning. The more emotional something is, the more likely we are to remember it.

Emotions are a critical part of our functioning in the world. Emotion helps us to assess quickly if something is a threat, and subsequently informs us to change our actions.

When something big happens in our world – when we have an experience that has a very positive or very negative effect – then we experience a strong emotion.

When we experience this strong emotion, it acts as a message to the brain, telling it to pay attention.

'This is important. Take note!'

'This is a threat/benefit to our survival; we want to move away from/towards this in the future.'

The intense emotions indicate significance, and this alerts the brain to create a strong neural network. All the firing creates strong wiring. So the more significant something is, the more likely the brain is to create strong connections around it. These connections – or shortcuts – are given priority in the brain. They can become our default ways of thinking and feeling in the corresponding situations, should they occur in the future. And the stronger and more often something fires, the deeper it wires.

Another way of looking at this is recognising that our emotions are like a current, and they give a charge or an energy to an experience.

Emotions speak directly to our *feeling* brain; they bypass our rational *thinking* brain. It could be argued that the *feeling* brain is the part which is really in charge, as our older *feeling* brain carries with it the years of evolution.

Quite simply from an evolutionary perspective, emotions help us to survive. They add a charge and sense of urgency to what we perceive in the world.

You know those times when you're stressed or in a fear state over something and you view the world through the lens of fear? While it's just your *feeling* brain wanting you to be extra cautious and stay safe, it affects all your interactions with the world. In this state, you are more inclined to say 'no,' and you feel worried, nervous, closed to possibility. You might say you're in a state of contraction. And your thoughts are tinged with this contraction.

Likewise, you know those times where you feel high on life? Or, you know, high in the '70s sense of the word – either way, in this state you are more inclined to 'yes.' You feel open to possibility, expectant, excited. You might say you are in a state of expansion or openness. And your thoughts are amplified with this feeling of expansion.

So which thoughts do you want to amplify?

The ones that feel like a 'no'?

Or the ones that feel like a 'yes'?

By consciously tapping into the power of evolution that is our *feeling* brain, we can amplify the 'fuck yes' feelings and make magic happen.

What If We Started Consciously Telling Our Brain Which Specific Connections to Make?

Given that a strong emotional reaction creates firing and wiring in our brain, it follows that if we add emotions to the new thoughts we want to connect with and embody, these new thoughts will wire much more quickly into our brains as new beliefs.

In amplifying our thoughts with emotions, we can effectively create new beliefs.

With this in mind, we can build and flex our 'fuck yes' muscle!

Do You Spend More Time Thinking About Your Past or Your Future?

Pause for a moment here. Put this book down and go back over your day so far and the thoughts that it has contained. Were there more thoughts about your past or your future?

For me here as I write, it's only 7:28am and I'm still in bed – perks of being your own boss. But so far this morning I've thought about the incident which happened the other day with our alpacas and the neighbour's dogs. I've thought about my effing patterns of procrastination and people pleasing, and I've thought about the fun night we had at a friend's party – and these are just the thoughts I'm conscious of!

Not much future thinking there, hey? And not much positivity, either – bar the party!

Shortly I will get up and do some exercise and affirmations. This is a conscious choice to be in my future, but the default for most of us, myself included, is spending more mental time in the stories of our past rather than in the creation of our future.

Our past is the container of our identity. It is the known. It is a safe space for our brain.

Our future, on the other hand, is the container of who we are yet to become. It is the unknown. And it is potentially an unsafe space for our brain – a brain that is obsessed with our survival.

Obsessed with surviving, not thriving.

Don't Just Collect 'Fuck Yes' Moments – Create Them

Once the possibilities were opened to me in my awkward adolescence, I was drawn to whatever I could get my hands on. And I've tried it all. I made vision boards, I visualised, I did 'cosmic ordering.' I followed all the fads of LOA. And sure, I got results, just enough little boosts to keep me believing and keep me trying.

However, the big things failed me. I found when I spent time visualising and thinking about my desires, half the time I would get stuck in a thinking loop of 'Um, but how the fuck is this going to happen again?' It all felt like too much work.

But I knew this was where the magic lived, and so I decided to play with it a little. I began tapping into the same energy as my 'fuck yes' moments and found that I could apply that 'fuck yes' *feeling* to the *thought* of some of my desires.

My 'fuck yes' wiring was so strong that I could easily tap into that feeling and attach it to a not yet realised 'fuck yes'.

Just the feeling. I resisted any thoughts that went into details around 'how the fuck will this eventuate?!'

I focused on just staying in that feeling, allowing the high vibe permission to anchor in my desire. But the key here is that I created an amplified feeling within a very short time. I'm talking seconds. I would spend mere seconds in that feeling and then I would move on and go about my day. Rather than meditating and visualising and so on, I just had an intense amplified feeling around the thought.

I figured if I could turn the feeling up, then I could spend less time on the thoughts themselves. Less time visualising and all that jazz. Instead, I just did a quick 'va-voom' of 'fuck yes!'

For me, this is the quickest way to manifest something. And with its speed, it enables me to avoid falling into the abyss of 'but how the fuck...?!'

Avoiding the Abyss of 'But How the Fuck?!'

Standing on one leg and pulling my boots on, I quickly gave myself a once over in the mirror by my front door.

Hair – check.

Earrings – check.

Teeth – check.

I grabbed the beanie from the corner of the mirror and pulled it over my head.

The picture at the bottom of the mirror caught my eye. I paused and smiled. It was a picture of me with my goddaughter and her brother, ages 1 and 3. They were both little blondies like myself, and we were often mistaken for family when I hung out with them. I imagined one day cuddling my own little cuties and loving them as much as I loved my goddaughter.

Can't wait to have my own cuties. Fuck yes!

At this thought, a huge wave of emotion travelled through my body. The pure feeling of this being my reality one day felt so good.

Straightening up, I applied lip gloss, grabbed my bag, and left my tiny London shoebox.

As I walked from my front door into the hustle and bustle of central London, I didn't give it any more thought. Even though I didn't have a boyfriend and I had no idea when I would in fact get my own cuties, there was a deep belief that I would. I was in my 30s and aware of some white noise about my biological clock, so it would have been easy for me to fall into fear around this.

But I knew that if every time I looked at that picture, I stayed in thoughts about it, then I would start to spiral down into the abyss of 'but how the fuck?!' I also knew that if I spent too long visualising this, the 'but hows?' would grab my blonde ass and drag me into their abyss.

Can't wait to have my own cuties...

Um, but how? You don't even have a boyfriend?

Your biological clock is ticking!

You would need to know someone for at least two years before deciding to have children, and then you'll be mid-thirties. That's old.

Tick tock.

Plus, you'll be tired by then.

Tick tock.

You'll be an old, tired mum.

So instead of following these *thoughts* down the spiral and into the abyss of 'but how the fuck?!,' I tapped into, and stayed in, the *feeling*. Then I moved on before the BHTFs could grab hold of me.

There were times that I would consciously still spend a longer time visualising and visioning this as my future, but if there was any hint of the BHTFs raising their ugly heads, then I'd stop straight away. I did not want to engage with or entertain these thoughts.

This is where you need to be super aware of your thoughts when you are visualising, and I think it's why many people give up on the powerful practise of visualisation. It falls into the 'too hard' basket.

But this is only because you are letting the BHTFs taint your otherwise high vibe thoughts. And if you aren't policing your thoughts like a mofo, then they can sneak in and do their damage before you can say 'Bob's your uncle.'

Anyway, a few months later I was dressed as a fairy on a stall at a raw food festival – as you do – and I felt someone looking at me.

I looked around and there, across the courtyard, was a man taking pictures of me. Having worked the music festivals as a fairy for a few summers, I wasn't camera shy, and I may or may not have pulled a few poses for him. Eventually he put his camera down and came over.

He was dressed in black skinny jeans with a chunky belt, loose T-shirt, and jean jacket; from his neck hung a plethora of Billy T-style chunky chains, and he somehow managed to pull off a mullet. He looked like he should be thrashing an electric guitar.

He so wasn't my type. I was more into a hipster vinyl-stroking vibe.

But he smiled and I smiled and we started talking. And even though he wasn't my type, I just wanted to keep talking to him. He made me feel something. Something that I hadn't felt in a long, long time. Something that was more than a tingle in my pants. Something that felt more like a flash of a nebula in my rib cage.

So we went on a date. We shared travel stories, dipped into family history, and bonded over our music tastes – turns out he had an amazing vinyl collection and DJ decks and had never touched an electric guitar in his life.

And the nebula flash grew into a little cosmos.

But towards the end of the evening he turned to me and said:

'I don't want to get married or have children.'

Whoa, that came out of nowhere. Um, I wasn't proposing; slow down, tiger.

Of course, I knew he was just letting me know what page he was on, so I let him know mine.

'Oh, really? I definitely want kids.'

But the energy between us was palatable, so we laughed and between the lines agreed to 'just have some fun.'

So fun we had. Fun speckled with a few conversations about our different desires for the future. And due to our differing desires, we developed a running joke about breaking up 'next Thursday'.

But a good few Thursdays later we were still together, and I started feeling the winds of change. London was all of a sudden smoky and I was craving fresher air. This confused me because I loved London.

Why do I want to leave? This is my favourite city in the whole world! Why do I feel like the air quality is not good? This has never bothered me before.

Then shark week never arrived.

My surfboard was ready, but the crimson wave never appeared.

Where the fuck was Aunt Flo?

Yes, a good few Thursdays later I was, in fact, defying all odds – and contraception. Pregnant. Thus explaining the winds of change and the desiring of air that wasn't polluted by eight million other inhabitants.

Conveniently, the moment I told Pete was the moment he realised he did in fact want to be a father.

Exceptional timing, Pete. Thank fuck for that.

And eight months later, in the living room of our 'next to the tube line ground floor flat,' I gave birth to our own little blondie.

Fuck yes.

- - -

Who knows what happens in the parallel universe, where each time I saw the photo of my goddaughter I was sucked into the 'abyss of hows.' But I would be willing to bet my future Tesla on the outcome being pretty different.

So now that I know the power of the 'fuck yes', I apply it to all my desires:

Lying by our pool under a big umbrella, watching the girls playing – fuck yes.

Sipping my handcrafted gin with botanicals from our garden – fuck yes.

Driving my Tesla – fuck yes.

Our mortgage paid off and holding the title for our house – fuck yes.

Doing a champagne tour in France – fuck yes.

Cutting loose at Burning Man – fuck yes.

My affirmations impacting people all over the world – fuck yes.

Charge Up Your Affirmations

If we add words to our affirmations that make us feel fierce and full of power, it follows that our affirmations are going to feel full of power. This will change our brain state and start firing and wiring in these new beliefs.

So find a word – one that is emotionally charged for you. A word that makes you smile – a full-bodied, eye-sparkling, fireworks in your rib cage kind of smile.

A word that when you hear it you get a surge of energy, a rush of feelgood, a 'va-voom' of emotion.

For me that word begins with F.

F. U. C. K.

This word is very emotionally charged for me – in my culture and in my life. Using this word is a sure-fire way and a quick hack for me to jump into the headspace of 'awesome,' of 'damn girl you've got this,' and of 'fuck yes'.

Adding in the emotion intrinsic to this word when I say my affirmations results in more neurons firing together, which of course means they will wire together.

And when they wire together, then they are becoming my new normal.

Fuck yes!

★

The small train came to a shuddering halt; relief and exhilaration clouded the faces of the people who had just been on the ride.

Once they were off, the attendant unhooked the rope barrier on our side and guided us to our seats. Only myself and one of my three younger brothers met the height restrictions, so my mother waited it out and our father accompanied us. Each 'rocket' was single file; my brother went in front, then myself, and then our father behind us.

We were secured in and the coaster slowly moved into the darkness. Lights flashed and we were counted down as if we were about to launch into space. My excitement and slight nausea built. We slowly started to ascend and then with a lurch we were off – catapulted into the darkness. The speed increased, the pitch black punctuated by flashing lights and strange sounds. We were jerked one way and then quickly twisted another. I squealed and laughed at each unexpected turn. My brother was also giggling and screaming. This was so much fun.

But then I became aware of my father behind me.

'Shit. Shit. Shit.' He said this quietly, almost under his breath. I couldn't quite believe what I was hearing. The most I had ever heard him swear was 'Jesus Christ.' The shock of this was greater than the thrill of the ride. And now, in the remembering of this story, I wonder if this is what created such a strong wiring for me at the time, what now makes this my one memory from that trip.

Perhaps I've created some kind of association between swearing and that feeling of exhilaration, or perhaps this memory stands out because of the significance. Either way, and perhaps thanks to Mr Disney, swearing is now one of my quickest ways to reach an amplified state.

But I know I'm not alone in this.

When I first came up with *F-Bomb Affirmations*, I realised that it might not sit well with everyone, so I started looking for research to support these bold claims I was making about swearing.

I was quite naturally delighted when I found that studies have indeed been done on the effects of swearing.

And research shows that swearing is in fact linked to our emotions.

You'll recall from Chapter 1 how we discussed the brain, and that it is divided into two areas, the left and right hemispheres. Within each hemisphere there are specific areas. The left hemisphere is home to language development. And the right hemisphere is home to emotional development.

Guess which part of the brain lights up when we swear?

The right. Swearing feels highly emotive.

Additionally, it has been found that swearing utilises many parts of the brain – parts of the brain where we process emotions, aka the *feeling* brain, and parts of the brain where cognitive processing happens, aka the *thinking* brain.

So swearing could be the ultimate bridge between the *feeling* and *thinking* brains.

But perhaps most intriguing of all, swearing has been found to be positively correlated with honesty.

Feldman et al., published a wonderful study in 2017 cleverly titled 'Frankly, We Do Give a Damn.' One of the reasons this line from *Gone with the Wind* was so memorable was because of the impact it had at the time. This moment in the film is where Rhett Butler passionately expresses his feelings. This moment cost the production company a whopping $5,000 fine for violating the Motion Picture Production Code for its use of this language. This moment is a perfect example of the contrasting opinions we had, and still have to some extent, towards swearing. It is seen, in the words of my father, as 'uncouth'.

However, back to the study. Feldman et al. conducted three experiments to explore the relationship between profanity and honesty. They found not only a strong relationship between swearing and honesty between individuals, but also that swearing was positively correlated with higher integrity at a societal level.

In their first experiment, they asked subjects to list their favourite and most used swear words and then gave them a lie test. They found that those who knew and used more swear words were less likely to lie.

In their second experiment, they collected data from 73,000 Facebook users. After analysis, they found that those who used more swear words in their online interactions were more likely to use language patterns related to honesty.

Their last study, and to me the most fascinating, is the comparison of swearing by state – i.e. in which states do the people who swear the most live – to what they called 'State Level Integrity.' They used an index of integrity to assess each state. This included things such as the state government's stance on honesty and transparency, the presence of ethics commissions, and executive, legislative, and judicial accountability. They found that the states that scored the highest on the integrity index were also the states with a higher level of swearing.

This supports the premise that swearing is often used to express our truest feelings, and aligns with the collective understanding that swearing comes from a place of honesty.

Swearing adds emphasis. Swearing is a strong word that indicates passion or truth. It is a shortcut for communicating something with urgency and passion.

The dictionary definition of swearing mentions two things – the taking of an oath and the use of offensive language. Wiktionary tells me that the second definition came after the first. So, there was some link here between taking an oath and using strong language. Perhaps a link between that intense feeling when you take an oath and the emphasis of a swear word.

'It offends me that you think I'm not telling the truth.'

When someone questions our integrity, it sparks an outrage, an anger, and it can fire us up. Fire us up so much that we get angry enough to use some strong language.

But I digress.

What Happens If We Add a Swear Word to Our Affirmations?

When we add a swear word to our affirmations, we engage both sides of the brain – left and right – and both 'brains' – *feeling* and *thinking*.

When we add a swear word to our affirmations, we tap into the collective correlation of swearing to honesty and passion.

When we add a swear word to our affirmations, we add a shite load of emphasis to the command we're giving our brain.

When we add a swear word to our affirmations, we utilise the power of emotions – emotions are indicators of significance. And significance indicates to our brain should make note and 'wire this in good now.'

When we add a swear word to our affirmations, we tap into the feeling of fierce that a swear word brings.

When we add a swear word to our affirmations, we create the ultimate bridge between our *feeling* and our *thinking* brains.

It could be argued that you could add another power word to your affirmations, and by all means go ahead – although if you're reading this book, it's likely that you resonate with swearing and are partial to an f-bomb here and there. If you use another non-swear word, it is unlikely you will be engaging your whole brain or tapping into the collective culture. So I say stick to the swear words.

Swearing is powerful because it brings with it a whole heap of beliefs. It fast-tracks you to some very strong wiring. It brings with it the energy of the collective culture. It taps into our fierce, our bad girl, and it tells our 'nice girl' where the fuck to go.

No matter what gender we identify with, most of us have a 'nice girl' inside. This is the part of us that was told to 'be nice' and 'be good'. This loosely defined archetype was something to aspire to, to please those around us. But this comes at a cost. The cost is our fierce, our strength – these are squashed in our pursuit of 'nice girl'. Nice girl cannot co-exist with fierce.

So tell her where the F to go, and get your fierce on.

Your Turn

Add an f-bomb to your affirmations:

Every day in every fucking way I am getting better and better.

Notice where you add it and how the emphasis changes:

Every fucking day in every way I am getting better and better.

Everyday day in every way I am getting fucking better and better.

Everyday fucking day in every fucking way I am getting better and better.

You get the idea...

Play With It

Try some other words. What other words give you that rush of 'fierce and feelgood'?

You can also try 'I feel fucking fantastic about...'

I feel fucking fantastic about my six-figure income.

I feel fucking amazing when I think about my new car.

I feel fucking amazing when I see my self as socially confident.

I feel fucking amazing when I see my self in the best health.

You could also try embracing the 'fuck yes' philosophy in all parts of your life – even the shite parts. Welcome it all, with your power and your fierce.

Fuck yes brings with it the element energy of 'can do' or 'I've got this.'

Get Curious

Ask some 'how' questions to shift out of the feelings and into the thoughts.

What Comes Up?

Sometimes we can feel like our fierce eludes us. Or it can bring with it some fear about claiming that space.

Journal your past fuck yes moments. Then list your future fuck yes moments. Tap into that feeling. How fucking good is that going to feel!?

Lying by the pool, cold beer in hand, my fave tunes playing, platter of cheese – fuck yes.

Sitting in a tiny cafe somewhere in Italy, known to the owners as I frequent there, having just placed my entire order and made small talk in Italian – fuck yes.

Opening up my emails to a beautiful review from someone who has read my book – fuck yes.

Imagine

Think of your favourite memory, a time where you felt on fire, full of love, full of life, a real fuck yes moment. Recall everything you can about this moment, what the weather was like, the temperature in the air, anything you smelt, what you saw, what you heard, and what you felt.

What feelings do you recall in this moment?

What made this a fuck yes moment?

Now let's go to a future fuck yes moment.

See yourself in this moment. What is the weather like? The temperature and quality of the air? What do you smell? What does this moment smell like? What does this moment sound like? What does this moment FEEL like?

Really allow the feelings in this moment to arise from deep inside you, that secret place where hope lives. Where anything and everything is possible. Allow these feelings to bloom. Give these feelings permission to bloom. Know that it is safe and you are worthy of these feelings. How freaking amazing does this moment feel?

Hack It Daily

Embrace your fierce.

Give yourself a pep talk in the mirror. It can be confronting to address yourself, but fuck, can it be powerful!

Curate and create your 'fuck yes' moments.

And as well as big fuck yes moments, practice cultivating your small daily ones. Some of mine these days are the little pleasures – fresh flowers, baby mangos, a Sunday arvo dance, a new gin.

Choose key words from an affirmation related to a current goal and use them as your passwords for logins you use often, e.g. '100%perfecthealth' or '6figureimpact!' or 'maldives2020!' If it's a shared login, you may want to use discretion. The first time I did this was in the '90s when writing my thesis; my supervisor looked at me oddly when he needed to access my work and I told him '2000-theyearitraveltheworld' was my password.

Get two Post-it notes. On one write a current goal. On the other write 'FUCK YES!'. Stick them both to a bottle of champagne. Keep the bottle in your fridge, so it's chilled and ready to pop once you reach your goal. Each time you see it imagine how freaking good it is going to feel popping that cork once you've hit your goal. *Fuck yes.*

Too Long; Didn't Read

- Emotions are indicators of significance and play an important role in the firing and wiring of beliefs.
- Create a life of 'fuck yes' moments.
- When you are thinking about your desires, don't get sucked into the abyss of 'but how the fuck?!'
- Swearing utilises many parts of the brain.
- Swearing is correlated with honesty.
- Use a swear word to add power to your affirmations.

THE END, BUT IT'S REALLY JUST THE BEGINNING...

I'm sitting at a new-to-me cafe in Golden Beach, right over the road from the sea. The tide is in and the water is the most unreal pale turquoise. There's a slight breeze and on it floats that ripe salty smell which takes me back to childhood summer holidays.

I never come down this end of the coast, so I kind of feel like I *am* on holiday. The decor is a Mediterranean blue and white; I could almost be in some tiny fishing village on an unpopulated coast of a forgotten Greek Island. It's a Friday lunchtime, and looking around, I realise I'm the least grey-haired customer, and the youngest by a few decades.

I am here to write the end of this book, for tomorrow I am sending the first draft to my beta readers. Excitement and nerves shimmy inside me in a strange, uncoordinated tango.

The end of this book!

It feels so unreal to type that and, in fact, to be at the end.

But for you, I hope this is just the beginning.

For you can apply the concepts in this book to all areas of your life.

Before we end, I want to bring your awareness to two things – the importance of feeling the not so happy feelings as well as the happy ones, and where to go from here.

Feeling All the Feels

As we have discussed throughout this book, and especially in the last chapter, emotions and emotional expression are an essential part of the human experience.

Even the negative ones – the ugly crying at 3am ones, the slamming-the-door-on-your-way-out ones, and the writing-a-letter-to-your-local-politician ones.

The idea isn't to bypass those strong and perhaps negative feelings in favour of the 'higher vibration' ones. Rather, we need to express these feelings. Remember, we need to 'feel it to heal it.'

Once we have felt and fully expressed the emotion, then we can start looking at the thoughts and stories behind the emotion. And then, with that awareness, we can choose to change our thoughts.

The key is to feel the emotions, but not to indulge them or let them get the better of us. Not to allow them to feed into more stories and to spiral down into darker feelings. We can use the feelings to heal, or we can stay in their negativity.

Are you going to indulge and let them feed your stories, so then they deepen, reinforce and fuel those stories? Like when something flops in your life and the emotions colour your internal dialogue:

Yep, well of course it was going to flop, it wasn't good enough, and that my darling, is because you aren't good enough, you tried, oh how you tried, but I'm afraid it just ain't up to scratch. This is you, this is how it is for you, I guess you thought things could be different...guess again, baby.

OR are you going to let them highlight and bring awareness to your stories so that you can heal and change them:

Huh, so this flopped, and I can feel it triggering my not-enough-ness, and that's interesting. Okay, some healing needs to happen there, so I can change this damn story!

When we reflect on the thoughts that got us to these heavier feelings, we can evaluate if they are part of a bigger story. If they are, then we need to ask ourselves if that story and believing and giving energy to that story, is helpful.

This takes awareness and discipline, but in changing our thoughts we can change the way we feel, and we can change our lives.

The term *spiritual bypassing* was coined in the '80s by Buddhist psychotherapist John Welwood. It refers to the tendency to use spirituality to bypass and avoid those feelings that make us feel uncomfortable or to avoid emotional wounds we may have.

This is where working on your limiting beliefs is important. And if you do discover something deeper, go on to reach out and seek some help in finding out what's underneath. This is where working with a therapist or coach can be helpful. I think a mandatory course of therapy annually would do wonders for the world!

All your feelings are valid. And that's what we are here for: to feel, and to heal.

Where To From Here?

Finishing a book is often a bittersweet thing. It can feel both satisfying and sad when you reach the end of the book and the words you read start to fade into or are muffled by the busy-ness of daily life.

Of course, we often leave a book feeling deeply inspired, but if we don't start implementing and reviewing what we have read, then we won't create the new neural networks we need to change our lives.

So, I encourage you to go back and do the exercises, to pick one a day and make it a part of your journaling practice. Print out the workbook from the website and fill it in completely. Make notes. Stick Post-it notes on your front door and on light switches; get some chalk markers and write on your bathroom mirror or even on your windows.

Do something every day to help rewire your brain.

Let's have a quick recap, the ultimate 'too long; didn't read,' if you will:

- Your *feeling* brain is powerful.
- Your biology is controlled by your beliefs.
- You can change your beliefs, and change your biology.

- As well as impacting your biology, your beliefs can impact the world.
- We can use our *thinking* brain to create new beliefs.
- Using language – especially affirmations – you can combine the power of your *feeling* brain and the power of your *thinking* brain to create the life you desire.
- And you now know how to:
    - Reassure your *feeling* brain that your desires are safe.
    - Give your whole being permission to have those desires.
    - Feel truly worthy of your desires.
    - Give gratitude for all that you have, now and in the future.
    - Feel your fucking power and use f-bombs to tap into the neurological power of emotion and the collective powers of passion and honesty.

So, my beauty, sprinkle f-bombs through all the parts of your life you want to imbue with that 'fuck yes' feeling. Collect and curate your fuck yes moments. Choose the best, most helpful thoughts. Know that you are safe. Give yourself permission. Feel your worth.

You have within you all the tools you need to create the life you desire.

Get the fuck out of your own way and make that shit happen.

Remember:

You are safe.

You are allowed.

You are worthy.

Go and be grateful for all the awesome in your life and all the awesome on its way.

And know that you are one fucking incredible human being.

With love and excitement,

Natalie x x x

GIMME MORE

The world is your fucking oyster.

So go make pearls, my lovely. And tell me about them! I love hearing how my affirmations change people's lives.

Drop me an email: hello@fbombaffirmations.com

Slide into my DMs: @fbombaffirmations on Instagram and Facebook.

Listen to my fave playlists: www.spotify.com/nataland-au

Get some f-bomb sprinkled affirmation tracks: www.fbombaffirmations.com/affirmation-recordings

Listen to my original affirmation tracks (no f-bombs): www.soundcloud.com/fbomb-affirmations

Learn how to easily incorporate affirmations into your daily life: www.fbombaffirmations.com/courses

ACKNOWLEDGMENTS

Bec from UnYucky, for the fortuitous meeting, instant connection, and accountability in the early days of our writing. Also for the introduction to book coach extraordinaire Cat Mora from Change Empire Books.

Without Cat, this book would still be in my head. Her feedback, support, knowledge, and gentle whip-cracking helped me to coax it out of my head and on to these pages.

My book coaching group. We did it, guys! Special thanks to Elysia for all the writing sprints and to Andrea and Mel in the last days as we raced to the finish line together.

My beta readers. Brooke, who agreed to be a beta reader with such enthusiasm, even though she later told me she had to google what a beta reader actually was. Alicia, for picking up on my incorrect grammar. Megan, for all the commas. Leanne, for adding and removing spaces where needed. And Emma, for reading with her characteristic depth and asking the right questions. Beyond the practical help, all of my beta readers were total cheerleaders and helped me to stay motivated to finish the book.

The talented Alexander Kent, for being so gracious and kind when I reached out to him about his art, and for allowing me to use his beautiful image for the cover of my book. Find more of his awesomeness www.alexander-kent.com.

Wonder editor Makenzi Crouch, for her amazing and efficient editing skills.

Hammad Khalid, for working his magic and getting the formatting on point.

My darling daughters: they light my world up, and I am so grateful they chose me to be their mama.

My beloved Pete, for all the support, laughs, and orgasms. He makes life so much more fun.

And, lastly, all my SoundCloud subscribers and listeners, whose mere presence gave me the encouragement I needed to start going public about dropping some f-bombs into my affirmations.

www.ingramcontent.com/pod-product-compliance
Lightning Source LLC
Chambersburg PA
CBHW020321010526
44107CB00054B/1929